TEACHER'S PET PUBLICATIONS

PUZZLE PACK™
for
From the Mixed-Up Files
of Mrs. Basil E. Frankweiler

based on the book by
E. L. Konigsburg

Written by
Mary B. Collins

© 2007 Teacher's Pet Publications
All Rights Reserved

The materials in this packet are copyrighted
by Teacher's Pet Publications, Inc.

These pages may be duplicated by the purchaser
for use in the purchaser's own classroom.

Copying any of these materials and distributing them
for any other purpose is a violation of the copyright laws.

© 2007 Teacher's Pet Publications, Inc.
www.tpet.com

INTRODUCTION
If you already own the LitPlan for this title, this Puzzle Pack will refresh your Unit Resource Materials and Vocabulary Resource Materials sections plus give you additional materials you can substitute into the tests. If you do not already have a complete LitPlan, these pages will give you some supplemental materials to use with your own plan. There are two main groups of materials: one set for unit words (such as characters' names, symbols, places, etc.) and one set for vocabulary words associated with the book.

WORD LIST
There is a word list for both the unit words and the vocabulary words. These lists show you which words are being used in the materials and the clues or definitions being used for those words. You may want to give students a word list with clues/definitions to help them, or you may want students to only have a word list (without clues/definitions) if you want them to work a little harder. Both are available for duplication. The word lists can also be your "calling key" for the bingo games.

FILL IN THE BLANK AND MATCHING
There are 4 each of the fill in the blank and matching worksheets for both the unit and vocabulary words. These pages can be used either as extra worksheets for students or as objective parts of a unit test. They can be done individually if students need extra help or as a whole class activity to review the material covered.

MAGIC SQUARES
The magic squares not only reinforce the material covered but also work on reasoning and math skills. Many teachers have told us that their students really enjoy doing these!

WORD SEARCH PUZZLES
The word search words go in all directions, as indicated on your answer keys. Two of the word search puzzles have the clues listed rather than the words. This makes the puzzle a little more difficult, but it reinforces the material better. Two word search puzzles have words only for students who find the clue puzzles too difficult.

CROSSWORD PUZZLES
Both unit and vocabulary word sections have 4 crossword puzzles.

BINGO CARDS
There are 32 individual bingo cards for the unit words and 32 individual bingo cards for the vocabulary words. You can use your word list as a "call list," calling the words at random and marking them off of your list as you go, or you could use the flash cards by cutting them apart and drawing the words at random from a hat (or box or whatever). To make a better review, you might ask for the definition and spelling of each word as you call it out–or you could call out the definitions and have students tell you the words they need to look for on the puzzle.

JUGGLE LETTERS
The vocabulary juggle letter game is intended to help students learn the spellings of the words. One sheet has the definitions listed on it as an extra help for students who need it or to reinforce the definitions if you choose to do so.

FLASH CARDS
We've included a set of vocabulary flash cards you can duplicate, cut, and fold for your students. Some teachers make a few sets for general use by the class; others make a set for each student. Some teachers duplicate them for each student and have the students cut & fold their own. You can cut out just the words and put them in a hat, have each student pick out one word and write the definition and a sentence for that word. Students then swap words and papers, with the next student adding a sentence of his own under the last one. You can have students swap as many times as you like. Each time the student will read the sentences written prior to his own and then add a sentence. You can cut out the words and definitions separately and play "I Have; Who Has?" Each student in the room draws a word and definition. The first student says, "I have (the name of the word). Who has the definition?" The student with the definition reads it then says, "I have (the name of the vocabulary word she has). Who has the definition?" The round continues until all words and definitions have been given.

Mixed Up Files Unit Word List

No.	Word	Clue/Definition
1.	ADOPT	The children plan to secretly _____ Mrs. Frankweiler.
2.	ANGEL	The statue with a secret.
3.	ATTORNEY	Occupation of Claudia and Jamie's grandfather.
4.	BRILLIANT	Jamie flatters Claudia by calling her ____.
5.	BRUCE	He plays cards with Jamie on the school bus.
6.	BUS	Claudia and Jamie skip school by hiding in the school _____.
7.	CEREAL	Claudia sends for a rebate from this type of company.
8.	CLAUDIA	She plans to run away.
9.	COINS	Jamie is carrying $24.43 worth of these in his pockets.
10.	DIFFERENT	Claudia wanted to return home this way.
11.	FARMINGTON	Town where Mrs. Frankweiler lives
12.	FIFTH	Strolling down _____ Avenue may cause Claudia to shop.
13.	FOUNTAIN	Place Claudia and Jamie bathe
14.	FRANKWEILER	Sold Angel to the Metropolitan Museum of Art
15.	HOMESICK	Being away from home is not making Claudia and Jamie ____.
16.	ITALY	The secret answer was found in the Bologna, ____ file.
17.	JAMIE	He makes extra money gambling at cards.
18.	KONIGSBURG	Author of From The Mixed Up Files of Mrs. Basil E. Frankweiler
19.	LAUNDRY	Claudia and Jamie run out of clean ____.
20.	LIBRARY	Place Claudia and Jamie go to research Michelangelo
21.	MET	Short for The Metropolitan Museum of Art
22.	MICHELANGELO	He created Angel.
23.	MIRROR	Mrs. Frankweiler asks Parks to bring her one.
24.	MONEY	Playing cards and the fountain are sources of this.
25.	MOTHER	Impossible thing Mrs. Frankweiler would like to be
26.	MUSEUM	Place Claudia and Jamie run away to
27.	ONE	Number of hours the kids have to find the secret.
28.	PARKS	Mrs. Frankweiler's butler
29.	PILLOW	Claudia places Jamie's instructions for running away here.
30.	PLANNING	Claudia's special talent
31.	ROLLS	The children are driven home in a ____ Royce.
32.	SARCOPHAGUS	Place Claudia hides her violin case
33.	SAXONBERG	Mrs. Frankweiler's lawyer
34.	SECRET	Claudia and Mrs. Frankweiler both like keeping these.
35.	SHELDON	Mrs. Frankweiler's driver
36.	SKETCH	Mrs. Frankweiler plans to bequeath this to the children.
37.	SMELLS	Claudia treasures good, clean ____.
38.	SONNET	One was written on the back of a sketch of Angel.
39.	STATUE	Jamie suggests fingerprinting this for clues.
40.	TAXI	How Claudia and Jamie travel to Farmington, Connecticut
41.	TRAIN	Claudia finds a _____ ticket in the wastebasket.
42.	UN	Claudia and Jamie take a tour of the ____.
43.	VELVET	Angel left three rings with an
44.	VIOLIN	Claudia uses her ____ case as a suitcase.
45.	WAR	Card game Jamie and Bruce play for money.

From the Mixed Up Files . . . Fill in the Blanks 1

_____

1. Claudia and Mrs. Frankweiler both like keeping these.
2. The children are driven home in a ____ Royce.
3. Author of From The Mixed Up Files of Mrs. Basil E. Frankweiler
4. Short for The Metropolitan Museum of Art
5. Claudia's special talent
6. Occupation of Claudia and Jamie's grandfather.
7. Town where Mrs. Frankweiler lives
8. The statue with a secret.
9. Place Claudia and Jamie bathe
10. Strolling down _____ Avenue may cause Claudia to shop.
11. Jamie suggests fingerprinting this for clues.
12. Mrs. Frankweiler's butler
13. He created Angel.
14. She plans to run away.
15. He plays cards with Jamie on the school bus.
16. Mrs. Frankweiler asks Parks to bring her one.
17. Claudia uses her ____ case as a suitcase.
18. Place Claudia hides her violin case
19. Claudia wanted to return home this way.
20. Mrs. Frankweiler's lawyer

From the Mixed Up Files . . . Fill in the Blanks 1 Answer Key

SECRET	1. Claudia and Mrs. Frankweiler both like keeping these.
ROLLS	2. The children are driven home in a ____ Royce.
KONIGSBURG	3. Author of From The Mixed Up Files of Mrs. Basil E. Frankweiler
MET	4. Short for The Metropolitan Museum of Art
PLANNING	5. Claudia's special talent
ATTORNEY	6. Occupation of Claudia and Jamie's grandfather.
FARMINGTON	7. Town where Mrs. Frankweiler lives
ANGEL	8. The statue with a secret.
FOUNTAIN	9. Place Claudia and Jamie bathe
FIFTH	10. Strolling down _____ Avenue may cause Claudia to shop.
STATUE	11. Jamie suggests fingerprinting this for clues.
PARKS	12. Mrs. Frankweiler's butler
MICHELANGELO	13. He created Angel.
CLAUDIA	14. She plans to run away.
BRUCE	15. He plays cards with Jamie on the school bus.
MIRROR	16. Mrs. Frankweiler asks Parks to bring her one.
VIOLIN	17. Claudia uses her ____ case as a suitcase.
SARCOPHAGUS	18. Place Claudia hides her violin case
DIFFERENT	19. Claudia wanted to return home this way.
SAXONBERG	20. Mrs. Frankweiler's lawyer

From the Mixed Up Files . . . Fill in the Blanks 2

_____ 1. Place Claudia hides her violin case
_____ 2. Claudia and Jamie skip school by hiding in the school _____.
_____ 3. Angel left three rings with an
_____ 4. Mrs. Frankweiler's lawyer
_____ 5. The children are driven home in a ____ Royce.
_____ 6. One was written on the back of a sketch of Angel.
_____ 7. Mrs. Frankweiler's butler
_____ 8. Number of hours the kids have to find the secret.
_____ 9. He created Angel.
_____ 10. Claudia finds a_____ ticket in the wastebasket.
_____ 11. He makes extra money gambling at cards.
_____ 12. Claudia wanted to return home this way.
_____ 13. Claudia treasures good, clean ____.
_____ 14. Strolling down _____ Avenue may cause Claudia to shop.
_____ 15. Place Claudia and Jamie go to research Michelangelo
_____ 16. Sold Angel to the Metropolitan Museum of Art
_____ 17. Playing cards and the fountain are sources of this.
_____ 18. He plays cards with Jamie on the school bus.
_____ 19. Place Claudia and Jamie run away to
_____ 20. Mrs. Frankweiler's driver

Copyrighted

From the Mixed Up Files . . . Fill in the Blanks 2 Answer Key

SARCOPHAGUS	1. Place Claudia hides her violin case
BUS	2. Claudia and Jamie skip school by hiding in the school _____.
VELVET	3. Angel left three rings with an
SAXONBERG	4. Mrs. Frankweiler's lawyer
ROLLS	5. The children are driven home in a ____ Royce.
SONNET	6. One was written on the back of a sketch of Angel.
PARKS	7. Mrs. Frankweiler's butler
ONE	8. Number of hours the kids have to find the secret.
MICHELANGELO	9. He created Angel.
TRAIN	10. Claudia finds a _____ ticket in the wastebasket.
JAMIE	11. He makes extra money gambling at cards.
DIFFERENT	12. Claudia wanted to return home this way.
SMELLS	13. Claudia treasures good, clean ____.
FIFTH	14. Strolling down _____ Avenue may cause Claudia to shop.
LIBRARY	15. Place Claudia and Jamie go to research Michelangelo
FRANKWEILER	16. Sold Angel to the Metropolitan Museum of Art
MONEY	17. Playing cards and the fountain are sources of this.
BRUCE	18. He plays cards with Jamie on the school bus.
MUSEUM	19. Place Claudia and Jamie run away to
SHELDON	20. Mrs. Frankweiler's driver

From the Mixed Up Files . . . Fill in the Blanks 3

_____ 1. He makes extra money gambling at cards.

_____ 2. Mrs. Frankweiler asks Parks to bring her one.

_____ 3. Claudia and Jamie run out of clean ____.

_____ 4. The secret answer was found in the Bologna, ____ file.

_____ 5. Claudia uses her ____ case as a suitcase.

_____ 6. Impossible thing Mrs. Frankweiler would like to be

_____ 7. Mrs. Frankweiler's butler

_____ 8. Strolling down ____ Avenue may cause Claudia to shop.

_____ 9. Jamie suggests fingerprinting this for clues.

_____ 10. The children are driven home in a ____ Royce.

_____ 11. One was written on the back of a sketch of Angel.

_____ 12. Claudia's special talent

_____ 13. The statue with a secret.

_____ 14. Claudia places Jamie's instructions for running away here.

_____ 15. Angel left three rings with an

_____ 16. Occupation of Claudia and Jamie's grandfather.

_____ 17. How Claudia and Jamie travel to Farmington, Connecticut

_____ 18. Mrs. Frankweiler plans to bequeath this to the children.

_____ 19. Card game Jamie and Bruce play for money.

_____ 20. Sold Angel to the Metropolitan Museum of Art

From the Mixed Up Files . . . Fill in the Blanks 3 Answer Key

JAMIE	1. He makes extra money gambling at cards.
MIRROR	2. Mrs. Frankweiler asks Parks to bring her one.
LAUNDRY	3. Claudia and Jamie run out of clean ____.
ITALY	4. The secret answer was found in the Bologna, ____ file.
VIOLIN	5. Claudia uses her ____ case as a suitcase.
MOTHER	6. Impossible thing Mrs. Frankweiler would like to be
PARKS	7. Mrs. Frankweiler's butler
FIFTH	8. Strolling down ____ Avenue may cause Claudia to shop.
STATUE	9. Jamie suggests fingerprinting this for clues.
ROLLS	10. The children are driven home in a ____ Royce.
SONNET	11. One was written on the back of a sketch of Angel.
PLANNING	12. Claudia's special talent
ANGEL	13. The statue with a secret.
PILLOW	14. Claudia places Jamie's instructions for running away here.
VELVET	15. Angel left three rings with an
ATTORNEY	16. Occupation of Claudia and Jamie's grandfather.
TAXI	17. How Claudia and Jamie travel to Farmington, Connecticut
SKETCH	18. Mrs. Frankweiler plans to bequeath this to the children.
WAR	19. Card game Jamie and Bruce play for money.
FRANKWEILER	20. Sold Angel to the Metropolitan Museum of Art

From the Mixed Up Files . . . Fill in the Blanks 4

_____ 1. Impossible thing Mrs. Frankweiler would like to be

_____ 2. The statue with a secret.

_____ 3. Card game Jamie and Bruce play for money.

_____ 4. Mrs. Frankweiler's butler

_____ 5. Occupation of Claudia and Jamie's grandfather.

_____ 6. Place Claudia and Jamie run away to

_____ 7. Being away from home is not making Claudia and Jamie ____.

_____ 8. Claudia wanted to return home this way.

_____ 9. Mrs. Frankweiler plans to bequeath this to the children.

_____ 10. Claudia finds a _____ ticket in the wastebasket.

_____ 11. She plans to run away.

_____ 12. Place Claudia hides her violin case

_____ 13. Jamie flatters Claudia by calling her ____.

_____ 14. Angel left three rings with an

_____ 15. He plays cards with Jamie on the school bus.

_____ 16. Place Claudia and Jamie bathe

_____ 17. Number of hours the kids have to find the secret.

_____ 18. Claudia uses her ____ case as a suitcase.

_____ 19. Claudia and Jamie take a tour of the ____.

_____ 20. Claudia and Jamie skip school by hiding in the school _____.

From the Mixed Up Files . . . Fill in the Blanks 4 Answer Key

MOTHER	1. Impossible thing Mrs. Frankweiler would like to be
ANGEL	2. The statue with a secret.
WAR	3. Card game Jamie and Bruce play for money.
PARKS	4. Mrs. Frankweiler's butler
ATTORNEY	5. Occupation of Claudia and Jamie's grandfather.
MUSEUM	6. Place Claudia and Jamie run away to
HOMESICK	7. Being away from home is not making Claudia and Jamie ____.
DIFFERENT	8. Claudia wanted to return home this way.
SKETCH	9. Mrs. Frankweiler plans to bequeath this to the children.
TRAIN	10. Claudia finds a _____ ticket in the wastebasket.
CLAUDIA	11. She plans to run away.
SARCOPHAGUS	12. Place Claudia hides her violin case
BRILLIANT	13. Jamie flatters Claudia by calling her ____.
VELVET	14. Angel left three rings with an
BRUCE	15. He plays cards with Jamie on the school bus.
FOUNTAIN	16. Place Claudia and Jamie bathe
ONE	17. Number of hours the kids have to find the secret.
VIOLIN	18. Claudia uses her ____ case as a suitcase.
UN	19. Claudia and Jamie take a tour of the ____.
BUS	20. Claudia and Jamie skip school by hiding in the school _____.

From the Mixed Up Files . . . Matching 1

___ 1. SHELDON   A. Claudia's special talent
___ 2. ONE   B. Claudia and Jamie run out of clean ____.
___ 3. ROLLS   C. He makes extra money gambling at cards.
___ 4. DIFFERENT   D. Claudia wanted to return home this way.
___ 5. HOMESICK   E. Claudia places Jamie's instructions for running away here.
___ 6. CEREAL   F. Claudia treasures good, clean ____.
___ 7. ADOPT   G. The children are driven home in a ____ Royce.
___ 8. ATTORNEY   H. Place Claudia hides her violin case
___ 9. SONNET   I. Mrs. Frankweiler's driver
___10. PILLOW   J. Number of hours the kids have to find the secret.
___11. PARKS   K. Claudia finds a _____ ticket in the wastebasket.
___12. ANGEL   L. Claudia sends for a rebate from this type of company.
___13. JAMIE   M. Occupation of Claudia and Jamie's grandfather.
___14. SMELLS   N. The children plan to secretly ____ Mrs. Frankweiler.
___15. MIRROR   O. Place Claudia and Jamie run away to
___16. PLANNING   P. The statue with a secret.
___17. LIBRARY   Q. Mrs. Frankweiler asks Parks to bring her one.
___18. BRUCE   R. Being away from home is not making Claudia and Jamie ____.
___19. VIOLIN   S. Claudia uses her ____ case as a suitcase.
___20. SARCOPHAGUS   T. One was written on the back of a sketch of Angel.
___21. TRAIN   U. Jamie suggests fingerprinting this for clues.
___22. MUSEUM   V. Mrs. Frankweiler's butler
___23. ITALY   W. He plays cards with Jamie on the school bus.
___24. STATUE   X. Place Claudia and Jamie go to research Michelangelo
___25. LAUNDRY   Y. The secret answer was found in the Bologna, ____ file.

From the Mixed Up Files . . . Matching 1 Answer Key

I - 1. SHELDON
J - 2. ONE
G - 3. ROLLS
D - 4. DIFFERENT
R - 5. HOMESICK
L - 6. CEREAL
N - 7. ADOPT
M - 8. ATTORNEY
T - 9. SONNET
E -10. PILLOW
V -11. PARKS
P -12. ANGEL
C -13. JAMIE
F -14. SMELLS
Q -15. MIRROR
A -16. PLANNING
X -17. LIBRARY
W -18. BRUCE
S -19. VIOLIN
H -20. SARCOPHAGUS
K -21. TRAIN
O -22. MUSEUM
Y -23. ITALY
U -24. STATUE
B -25. LAUNDRY

A. Claudia's special talent
B. Claudia and Jamie run out of clean ____.
C. He makes extra money gambling at cards.
D. Claudia wanted to return home this way.
E. Claudia places Jamie's instructions for running away here.
F. Claudia treasures good, clean ____.
G. The children are driven home in a ____ Royce.
H. Place Claudia hides her violin case
I. Mrs. Frankweiler's driver
J. Number of hours the kids have to find the secret.
K. Claudia finds a _____ ticket in the wastebasket.
L. Claudia sends for a rebate from this type of company.
M. Occupation of Claudia and Jamie's grandfather.
N. The children plan to secretly _____ Mrs. Frankweiler.
O. Place Claudia and Jamie run away to
P. The statue with a secret.
Q. Mrs. Frankweiler asks Parks to bring her one.
R. Being away from home is not making Claudia and Jamie ____.
S. Claudia uses her ____ case as a suitcase.
T. One was written on the back of a sketch of Angel.
U. Jamie suggests fingerprinting this for clues.
V. Mrs. Frankweiler's butler
W. He plays cards with Jamie on the school bus.
X. Place Claudia and Jamie go to research Michelangelo
Y. The secret answer was found in the Bologna, ____ file.

From the Mixed Up Files . . . Matching 2

___ 1. UN
___ 2. HOMESICK
___ 3. STATUE
___ 4. BRILLIANT
___ 5. TRAIN
___ 6. FRANKWEILER
___ 7. VIOLIN
___ 8. MET
___ 9. BUS
___ 10. ADOPT
___ 11. FARMINGTON
___ 12. SONNET
___ 13. TAXI
___ 14. ROLLS
___ 15. COINS
___ 16. LIBRARY
___ 17. CLAUDIA
___ 18. SAXONBERG
___ 19. LAUNDRY
___ 20. MONEY
___ 21. FIFTH
___ 22. SMELLS
___ 23. ITALY
___ 24. PILLOW
___ 25. VELVET

A. Sold Angel to the Metropolitan Museum of Art
B. Playing cards and the fountain are sources of this.
C. Jamie suggests fingerprinting this for clues.
D. Claudia and Jamie take a tour of the ____.
E. Claudia and Jamie run out of clean ____.
F. Place Claudia and Jamie go to research Michelangelo
G. Claudia finds a _____ ticket in the wastebasket.
H. The children plan to secretly _____ Mrs. Frankweiler.
I. The secret answer was found in the Bologna, ____ file.
J. Jamie flatters Claudia by calling her ____.
K. Jamie is carrying $24.43 worth of these in his pockets.
L. Short for The Metropolitan Museum of Art
M. Town where Mrs. Frankweiler lives
N. Being away from home is not making Claudia and Jamie ____.
O. Claudia and Jamie skip school by hiding in the school ____.
P. The children are driven home in a ____ Royce.
Q. Strolling down _____ Avenue may cause Claudia to shop.
R. She plans to run away.
S. Claudia places Jamie's instructions for running away here.
T. How Claudia and Jamie travel to Farmington, Connecticut
U. One was written on the back of a sketch of Angel.
V. Mrs. Frankweiler's lawyer
W. Angel left three rings with an
X. Claudia uses her ____ case as a suitcase.
Y. Claudia treasures good, clean ____.

From the Mixed Up Files . . . Matching 2 Answer Key

D - 1. UN	A. Sold Angel to the Metropolitan Museum of Art
N - 2. HOMESICK	B. Playing cards and the fountain are sources of this.
C - 3. STATUE	C. Jamie suggests fingerprinting this for clues.
J - 4. BRILLIANT	D. Claudia and Jamie take a tour of the ____.
G - 5. TRAIN	E. Claudia and Jamie run out of clean ____.
A - 6. FRANKWEILER	F. Place Claudia and Jamie go to research Michelangelo
X - 7. VIOLIN	G. Claudia finds a ____ ticket in the wastebasket.
L - 8. MET	H. The children plan to secretly ____ Mrs. Frankweiler.
O - 9. BUS	I. The secret answer was found in the Bologna, ____ file.
H - 10. ADOPT	J. Jamie flatters Claudia by calling her ____.
M - 11. FARMINGTON	K. Jamie is carrying $24.43 worth of these in his pockets.
U - 12. SONNET	L. Short for The Metropolitan Museum of Art
T - 13. TAXI	M. Town where Mrs. Frankweiler lives
P - 14. ROLLS	N. Being away from home is not making Claudia and Jamie ____.
K - 15. COINS	O. Claudia and Jamie skip school by hiding in the school ____.
F - 16. LIBRARY	P. The children are driven home in a ____ Royce.
R - 17. CLAUDIA	Q. Strolling down ____ Avenue may cause Claudia to shop.
V - 18. SAXONBERG	R. She plans to run away.
E - 19. LAUNDRY	S. Claudia places Jamie's instructions for running away here.
B - 20. MONEY	T. How Claudia and Jamie travel to Farmington, Connecticut
Q - 21. FIFTH	U. One was written on the back of a sketch of Angel.
Y - 22. SMELLS	V. Mrs. Frankweiler's lawyer
I - 23. ITALY	W. Angel left three rings with an
S - 24. PILLOW	X. Claudia uses her ____ case as a suitcase.
W - 25. VELVET	Y. Claudia treasures good, clean ____.

From the Mixed Up Files . . . Matching 3

___ 1. ITALY
___ 2. COINS
___ 3. SONNET
___ 4. SHELDON
___ 5. MIRROR
___ 6. MICHELANGELO
___ 7. CLAUDIA
___ 8. PLANNING
___ 9. WAR
___ 10. VELVET
___ 11. PARKS
___ 12. ONE
___ 13. SKETCH
___ 14. MONEY
___ 15. JAMIE
___ 16. LAUNDRY
___ 17. KONIGSBURG
___ 18. FIFTH
___ 19. ATTORNEY
___ 20. LIBRARY
___ 21. MUSEUM
___ 22. BRUCE
___ 23. SARCOPHAGUS
___ 24. BRILLIANT
___ 25. HOMESICK

A. Strolling down _____ Avenue may cause Claudia to shop.
B. Claudia's special talent
C. Card game Jamie and Bruce play for money.
D. Place Claudia and Jamie run away to
E. Occupation of Claudia and Jamie's grandfather.
F. He makes extra money gambling at cards.
G. He created Angel.
H. Number of hours the kids have to find the secret.
I. Jamie is carrying $24.43 worth of these in his pockets.
J. Being away from home is not making Claudia and Jamie ____.
K. Author of From The Mixed Up Files of Mrs. Basil E. Frankweiler
L. Jamie flatters Claudia by calling her ____.
M. He plays cards with Jamie on the school bus.
N. Place Claudia and Jamie go to research Michelangelo
O. Mrs. Frankweiler plans to bequeath this to the children.
P. Mrs. Frankweiler's butler
Q. She plans to run away.
R. One was written on the back of a sketch of Angel.
S. Mrs. Frankweiler's driver
T. The secret answer was found in the Bologna, ____ file.
U. Claudia and Jamie run out of clean ____.
V. Playing cards and the fountain are sources of this.
W. Place Claudia hides her violin case
X. Mrs. Frankweiler asks Parks to bring her one.
Y. Angel left three rings with an

From the Mixed Up Files . . . Matching 3 Answer Key

T - 1. ITALY	A.	Strolling down _____ Avenue may cause Claudia to shop.
I - 2. COINS	B.	Claudia's special talent
R - 3. SONNET	C.	Card game Jamie and Bruce play for money.
S - 4. SHELDON	D.	Place Claudia and Jamie run away to
X - 5. MIRROR	E.	Occupation of Claudia and Jamie's grandfather.
G - 6. MICHELANGELO	F.	He makes extra money gambling at cards.
Q - 7. CLAUDIA	G.	He created Angel.
B - 8. PLANNING	H.	Number of hours the kids have to find the secret.
C - 9. WAR	I.	Jamie is carrying $24.43 worth of these in his pockets.
Y -10. VELVET	J.	Being away from home is not making Claudia and Jamie _____.
P -11. PARKS	K.	Author of From The Mixed Up Files of Mrs. Basil E. Frankweiler
H -12. ONE	L.	Jamie flatters Claudia by calling her _____.
O -13. SKETCH	M.	He plays cards with Jamie on the school bus.
V -14. MONEY	N.	Place Claudia and Jamie go to research Michelangelo
F -15. JAMIE	O.	Mrs. Frankweiler plans to bequeath this to the children.
U -16. LAUNDRY	P.	Mrs. Frankweiler's butler
K -17. KONIGSBURG	Q.	She plans to run away.
A -18. FIFTH	R.	One was written on the back of a sketch of Angel.
E -19. ATTORNEY	S.	Mrs. Frankweiler's driver
N -20. LIBRARY	T.	The secret answer was found in the Bologna, _____ file.
D -21. MUSEUM	U.	Claudia and Jamie run out of clean _____.
M -22. BRUCE	V.	Playing cards and the fountain are sources of this.
W -23. SARCOPHAGUS	W.	Place Claudia hides her violin case
L -24. BRILLIANT	X.	Mrs. Frankweiler asks Parks to bring her one.
J -25. HOMESICK	Y.	Angel left three rings with an

From the Mixed Up Files . . . Matching 4

___ 1. LIBRARY   A. He plays cards with Jamie on the school bus.
___ 2. VIOLIN   B. Card game Jamie and Bruce play for money.
___ 3. ADOPT   C. The children are driven home in a ____ Royce.
___ 4. ROLLS   D. Impossible thing Mrs. Frankweiler would like to be
___ 5. MET   E. Mrs. Frankweiler asks Parks to bring her one.
___ 6. VELVET   F. Sold Angel to the Metropolitan Museum of Art
___ 7. FARMINGTON   G. Claudia uses her ____ case as a suitcase.
___ 8. BRUCE   H. Place Claudia and Jamie go to research Michelangelo
___ 9. BRILLIANT   I. Playing cards and the fountain are sources of this.
___ 10. WAR   J. Author of From The Mixed Up Files of Mrs. Basil E. Frankweiler
___ 11. MICHELANGELO   K. Occupation of Claudia and Jamie's grandfather.
___ 12. SHELDON   L. Mrs. Frankweiler's lawyer
___ 13. FIFTH   M. The children plan to secretly _____ Mrs. Frankweiler.
___ 14. SAXONBERG   N. Strolling down _____ Avenue may cause Claudia to shop.
___ 15. MOTHER   O. Short for The Metropolitan Museum of Art
___ 16. TAXI   P. He makes extra money gambling at cards.
___ 17. MONEY   Q. Claudia and Jamie take a tour of the ____.
___ 18. KONIGSBURG   R. Claudia and Jamie skip school by hiding in the school _____.
___ 19. UN   S. Jamie flatters Claudia by calling her ____.
___ 20. JAMIE   T. He created Angel.
___ 21. BUS   U. How Claudia and Jamie travel to Farmington, Connecticut
___ 22. SECRET   V. Angel left three rings with an
___ 23. FRANKWEILER   W. Mrs. Frankweiler's driver
___ 24. ATTORNEY   X. Town where Mrs. Frankweiler lives
___ 25. MIRROR   Y. Claudia and Mrs. Frankweiler both like keeping these.

From the Mixed Up Files . . . Matching 4 Answer Key

H - 1. LIBRARY
G - 2. VIOLIN
M - 3. ADOPT
C - 4. ROLLS
O - 5. MET
V - 6. VELVET
X - 7. FARMINGTON
A - 8. BRUCE
S - 9. BRILLIANT
B - 10. WAR
T - 11. MICHELANGELO
W - 12. SHELDON
N - 13. FIFTH
L - 14. SAXONBERG
D - 15. MOTHER
U - 16. TAXI
I - 17. MONEY
J - 18. KONIGSBURG
Q - 19. UN
P - 20. JAMIE
R - 21. BUS
Y - 22. SECRET
F - 23. FRANKWEILER
K - 24. ATTORNEY
E - 25. MIRROR

A. He plays cards with Jamie on the school bus.
B. Card game Jamie and Bruce play for money.
C. The children are driven home in a ____ Royce.
D. Impossible thing Mrs. Frankweiler would like to be
E. Mrs. Frankweiler asks Parks to bring her one.
F. Sold Angel to the Metropolitan Museum of Art
G. Claudia uses her ____ case as a suitcase.
H. Place Claudia and Jamie go to research Michelangelo
I. Playing cards and the fountain are sources of this.
J. Author of From The Mixed Up Files of Mrs. Basil E. Frankweiler
K. Occupation of Claudia and Jamie's grandfather.
L. Mrs. Frankweiler's lawyer
M. The children plan to secretly ____ Mrs. Frankweiler.
N. Strolling down ____ Avenue may cause Claudia to shop.
O. Short for The Metropolitan Museum of Art
P. He makes extra money gambling at cards.
Q. Claudia and Jamie take a tour of the ____.
R. Claudia and Jamie skip school by hiding in the school ____.
S. Jamie flatters Claudia by calling her ____.
T. He created Angel.
U. How Claudia and Jamie travel to Farmington, Connecticut
V. Angel left three rings with an
W. Mrs. Frankweiler's driver
X. Town where Mrs. Frankweiler lives
Y. Claudia and Mrs. Frankweiler both like keeping these.

From the Mixed Up Files . . . Magic Squares 1

Match the definition with the vocabulary word. Put your answers in the magic squares below. When your answers are correct, all columns and rows will add to the same number.

A. FARMINGTON
B. MET
C. FIFTH
D. BUS
E. STATUE
F. MONEY
G. HOMESICK
H. LAUNDRY
I. ATTORNEY
J. ADOPT
K. CLAUDIA
L. PARKS
M. BRUCE
N. MUSEUM
O. SKETCH
P. JAMIE

1. Mrs. Frankweiler plans to bequeath this to the children.
2. The children plan to secretly _____ Mrs. Frankweiler.
3. Claudia and Jamie run out of clean _____.
4. Town where Mrs. Frankweiler lives
5. Claudia and Jamie skip school by hiding in the school _____.
6. Jamie suggests fingerprinting this for clues.
7. She plans to run away.
8. Place Claudia and Jamie run away to
9. Playing cards and the fountain are sources of this.
10. Strolling down _____ Avenue may cause Claudia to shop.
11. He plays cards with Jamie on the school bus.
12. Mrs. Frankweiler's butler
13. Occupation of Claudia and Jamie's grandfather.
14. He makes extra money gambling at cards.
15. Short for The Metropolitan Museum of Art
16. Being away from home is not making Claudia and Jamie _____.

A=	B=	C=	D=
E=	F=	G=	H=
I=	J=	K=	L=
M=	N=	O=	P=

From the Mixed Up Files . . . Magic Squares 1 Answer Key

Match the definition with the vocabulary word. Put your answers in the magic squares below. When your answers are correct, all columns and rows will add to the same number.

A. FARMINGTON
B. MET
C. FIFTH
D. BUS
E. STATUE
F. MONEY

G. HOMESICK
H. LAUNDRY
I. ATTORNEY
J. ADOPT
K. CLAUDIA
L. PARKS

M. BRUCE
N. MUSEUM
O. SKETCH
P. JAMIE

1. Mrs. Frankweiler plans to bequeath this to the children.
2. The children plan to secretly _____ Mrs. Frankweiler.
3. Claudia and Jamie run out of clean _____.
4. Town where Mrs. Frankweiler lives
5. Claudia and Jamie skip school by hiding in the school _____.
6. Jamie suggests fingerprinting this for clues.
7. She plans to run away.
8. Place Claudia and Jamie run away to
9. Playing cards and the fountain are sources of this.
10. Strolling down _____ Avenue may cause Claudia to shop.
11. He plays cards with Jamie on the school bus.
12. Mrs. Frankweiler's butler
13. Occupation of Claudia and Jamie's grandfather.
14. He makes extra money gambling at cards.
15. Short for The Metropolitan Museum of Art
16. Being away from home is not making Claudia and Jamie _____.

A=4	B=15	C=10	D=5
E=6	F=9	G=16	H=3
I=13	J=2	K=7	L=12
M=11	N=8	O=1	P=14

From the Mixed Up Files . . . Magic Squares 2

Match the definition with the vocabulary word. Put your answers in the magic squares below. When your answers are correct, all columns and rows will add to the same number.

A. MET
B. VELVET
C. TAXI
D. SMELLS
E. MUSEUM
F. COINS
G. CEREAL
H. WAR
I. DIFFERENT
J. ATTORNEY
K. BRUCE
L. PARKS
M. ROLLS
N. BUS
O. MICHELANGELO
P. PLANNING

1. Card game Jamie and Bruce play for money.
2. The children are driven home in a ____ Royce.
3. Angel left three rings with an
4. He plays cards with Jamie on the school bus.
5. Occupation of Claudia and Jamie's grandfather.
6. How Claudia and Jamie travel to Farmington, Connecticut
7. Claudia's special talent
8. Place Claudia and Jamie run away to
9. He created Angel.
10. Jamie is carrying $24.43 worth of these in his pockets.
11. Claudia wanted to return home this way.
12. Claudia treasures good, clean ____.
13. Short for The Metropolitan Museum of Art
14. Mrs. Frankweiler's butler
15. Claudia sends for a rebate from this type of company.
16. Claudia and Jamie skip school by hiding in the school ____.

A=	B=	C=	D=
E=	F=	G=	H=
I=	J=	K=	L=
M=	N=	O=	P=

From the Mixed Up Files . . . Magic Squares 2 Answer Key

Match the definition with the vocabulary word. Put your answers in the magic squares below. When your answers are correct, all columns and rows will add to the same number.

A. MET
B. VELVET
C. TAXI
D. SMELLS
E. MUSEUM
F. COINS
G. CEREAL
H. WAR
I. DIFFERENT
J. ATTORNEY
K. BRUCE
L. PARKS
M. ROLLS
N. BUS
O. MICHELANGELO
P. PLANNING

1. Card game Jamie and Bruce play for money.
2. The children are driven home in a ____ Royce.
3. Angel left three rings with an
4. He plays cards with Jamie on the school bus.
5. Occupation of Claudia and Jamie's grandfather.
6. How Claudia and Jamie travel to Farmington, Connecticut
7. Claudia's special talent
8. Place Claudia and Jamie run away to
9. He created Angel.
10. Jamie is carrying $24.43 worth of these in his pockets.
11. Claudia wanted to return home this way.
12. Claudia treasures good, clean ____.
13. Short for The Metropolitan Museum of Art
14. Mrs. Frankweiler's butler
15. Claudia sends for a rebate from this type of company.
16. Claudia and Jamie skip school by hiding in the school ____.

A=13	B=3	C=6	D=12
E=8	F=10	G=15	H=1
I=11	J=5	K=4	L=14
M=2	N=16	O=9	P=7

From the Mixed Up Files . . . Magic Squares 3

Match the definition with the vocabulary word. Put your answers in the magic squares below. When your answers are correct, all columns and rows will add to the same number.

A. BRUCE
B. STATUE
C. WAR
D. MIRROR
E. COINS
F. JAMIE
G. LAUNDRY
H. CEREAL
I. SKETCH
J. MONEY
K. FARMINGTON
L. KONIGSBURG
M. SMELLS
N. ROLLS
O. SHELDON
P. BUS

1. Claudia sends for a rebate from this type of company.
2. He plays cards with Jamie on the school bus.
3. Jamie suggests fingerprinting this for clues.
4. Claudia and Jamie run out of clean ____.
5. Playing cards and the fountain are sources of this.
6. Mrs. Frankweiler's driver
7. Claudia and Jamie skip school by hiding in the school _____.
8. Mrs. Frankweiler plans to bequeath this to the children.
9. Town where Mrs. Frankweiler lives
10. The children are driven home in a ____ Royce.
11. Claudia treasures good, clean ____.
12. Author of From The Mixed Up Files of Mrs. Basil E. Frankweiler
13. Jamie is carrying $24.43 worth of these in his pockets.
14. Mrs. Frankweiler asks Parks to bring her one.
15. Card game Jamie and Bruce play for money.
16. He makes extra money gambling at cards.

A=	B=	C=	D=
E=	F=	G=	H=
I=	J=	K=	L=
M=	N=	O=	P=

From the Mixed Up Files . . . Magic Squares 3 Answer Key

Match the definition with the vocabulary word. Put your answers in the magic squares below. When your answers are correct, all columns and rows will add to the same number.

A. BRUCE
B. STATUE
C. WAR
D. MIRROR
E. COINS
F. JAMIE
G. LAUNDRY
H. CEREAL
I. SKETCH
J. MONEY
K. FARMINGTON
L. KONIGSBURG
M. SMELLS
N. ROLLS
O. SHELDON
P. BUS

1. Claudia sends for a rebate from this type of company.
2. He plays cards with Jamie on the school bus.
3. Jamie suggests fingerprinting this for clues.
4. Claudia and Jamie run out of clean _____.
5. Playing cards and the fountain are sources of this.
6. Mrs. Frankweiler's driver
7. Claudia and Jamie skip school by hiding in the school _____.
8. Mrs. Frankweiler plans to bequeath this to the children.
9. Town where Mrs. Frankweiler lives
10. The children are driven home in a _____ Royce.
11. Claudia treasures good, clean _____.
12. Author of From The Mixed Up Files of Mrs. Basil E. Frankweiler
13. Jamie is carrying $24.43 worth of these in his pockets.
14. Mrs. Frankweiler asks Parks to bring her one.
15. Card game Jamie and Bruce play for money.
16. He makes extra money gambling at cards.

A=2	B=3	C=15	D=14
E=13	F=16	G=4	H=1
I=8	J=5	K=9	L=12
M=11	N=10	O=6	P=7

From the Mixed Up Files . . . Magic Squares 4

Match the definition with the vocabulary word. Put your answers in the magic squares below. When your answers are correct, all columns and rows will add to the same number.

A. LAUNDRY
B. VIOLIN
C. ATTORNEY
D. KONIGSBURG
E. SARCOPHAGUS
F. SMELLS
G. MOTHER
H. MONEY
I. ADOPT
J. FRANKWEILER
K. FIFTH
L. PILLOW
M. CEREAL
N. PLANNING
O. CLAUDIA
P. HOMESICK

1. Occupation of Claudia and Jamie's grandfather.
2. Sold Angel to the Metropolitan Museum of Art
3. Claudia treasures good, clean ____.
4. She plans to run away.
5. Being away from home is not making Claudia and Jamie ____.
6. Place Claudia hides her violin case
7. The children plan to secretly ____ Mrs. Frankweiler.
8. Author of From The Mixed Up Files of Mrs. Basil E. Frankweiler
9. Claudia sends for a rebate from this type of company.
10. Playing cards and the fountain are sources of this.
11. Claudia places Jamie's instructions for running away here.
12. Claudia and Jamie run out of clean ____.
13. Claudia uses her ____ case as a suitcase.
14. Strolling down ____ Avenue may cause Claudia to shop.
15. Impossible thing Mrs. Frankweiler would like to be
16. Claudia's special talent

A=	B=	C=	D=
E=	F=	G=	H=
I=	J=	K=	L=
M=	N=	O=	P=

From the Mixed Up Files . . . Magic Squares 4 Answer Key

Match the definition with the vocabulary word. Put your answers in the magic squares below. When your answers are correct, all columns and rows will add to the same number.

A. LAUNDRY
B. VIOLIN
C. ATTORNEY
D. KONIGSBURG
E. SARCOPHAGUS
F. SMELLS
G. MOTHER
H. MONEY
I. ADOPT
J. FRANKWEILER
K. FIFTH
L. PILLOW
M. CEREAL
N. PLANNING
O. CLAUDIA
P. HOMESICK

1. Occupation of Claudia and Jamie's grandfather.
2. Sold Angel to the Metropolitan Museum of Art
3. Claudia treasures good, clean ____.
4. She plans to run away.
5. Being away from home is not making Claudia and Jamie ____.
6. Place Claudia hides her violin case
7. The children plan to secretly _____ Mrs. Frankweiler.
8. Author of From The Mixed Up Files of Mrs. Basil E. Frankweiler
9. Claudia sends for a rebate from this type of company.
10. Playing cards and the fountain are sources of this.
11. Claudia places Jamie's instructions for running away here.
12. Claudia and Jamie run out of clean ____.
13. Claudia uses her ____ case as a suitcase.
14. Strolling down _____ Avenue may cause Claudia to shop.
15. Impossible thing Mrs. Frankweiler would like to be
16. Claudia's special talent

A=12	B=13	C=1	D=8
E=6	F=3	G=15	H=10
I=7	J=2	K=14	L=11
M=9	N=16	O=4	P=5

From the Mixed Up Files . . . Word Search 1

```
M G W B S A X O N B E R G T A X I C P Q
I Y M R Z H O M E S I C K L D L V E L X
R X L I Z K E M O T H E R I O F X R A Q
R C R L C D D L S G Y Z M B P A S E N H
O T O L Q H N F D N C T Q R T R H A N V
R G G I G K E X P O W L R A X M F L I N
W W R A N B L L K A N C O R X I C N N R
L F Y N B S R F A V R M L Y L N L N G Y
Z T L T X N T B L N D K L C P G A J S S
W J S A R C O P H A G U S T A T U E E C
T M A S X A Q V V P M E L Y F O D N C T
T V V M V N B M S I I M L A M N I J R H
F R E S I G R U X K O L U O U O A J E M
I T A L Y E U N S M E L L S O N N E T W
F W Z I V L C K B S E T I O E E D E W N
T A G R N E E G J P K T C N W U S R Y X
H R C Q A T T O R N E Y H H K M M F Y C
```

Angel left three rings with a W on this. (6)
Being away from home is not making Claudia and Jamie ____. (8)
Card game Jamie and Bruce play for money (3)
Claudia and Jamie run out of clean ____. (7)
Claudia and Jamie skip school by hiding in the school ____. (3)
Claudia and Jamie take a tour of the ____. (2)
Claudia and Mrs. Frankweiler both like keeping these. (6)
Claudia finds a ____ ticket in the wastebasket. (5)
Claudia places Jamie's instructions for running away here. (6)
Claudia sends for a rebate from this type of company. (6)
Claudia treasures good, clean ____. (6)
Claudia uses her ____ case as a suitcase. (6)
Claudia's special talent (8)
He created Angel. (12)
He makes extra money gambling at cards. (5)
He plays cards with Jamie on the school bus. (5)
How Claudia and Jamie travel to Farmington, Connecticut (4)
Impossible thing Mrs. Frankweiler would like to be (6)
Jamie flatters Claudia by calling her ____. (9)
Jamie is carrying $24.43 worth of these in his pockets. (5)
Jamie suggests fingerprinting this for clues. (6)
Mrs. Frankweiler asks Parks to bring her one. (6)

Mrs. Frankweiler plans to bequeath this to the children. (6)
Mrs. Frankweiler's butler (5)
Mrs. Frankweiler's driver (7)
Mrs. Frankweiler's lawyer (9)
Number of hours the kids have to find the secret (3)
Occupation of Claudia and Jamie's grandfather (8)
One was written on the back of a sketch of Angel. (6)
Place Claudia and Jamie go to research Michelangelo (7)
Place Claudia and Jamie run away to (6)
Place Claudia hides her violin case (11)
Playing cards and the fountain are sources of this. (5)
She plans to run away. (7)
Short for The Metropolitan Museum of Art (3)
Strolling down ____ Avenue may cause Claudia to shop. (5)
The children are driven home in a ____ Royce. (5)
The children plan to secretly ____ Mrs. Frankweiler. (5)
The secret answer was found in the Bologna, ____ file. (5)
The statue with a secret (5)
Town where Mrs. Frankweiler lives (10)

From the Mixed Up Files . . . Word Search 1 Answer Key

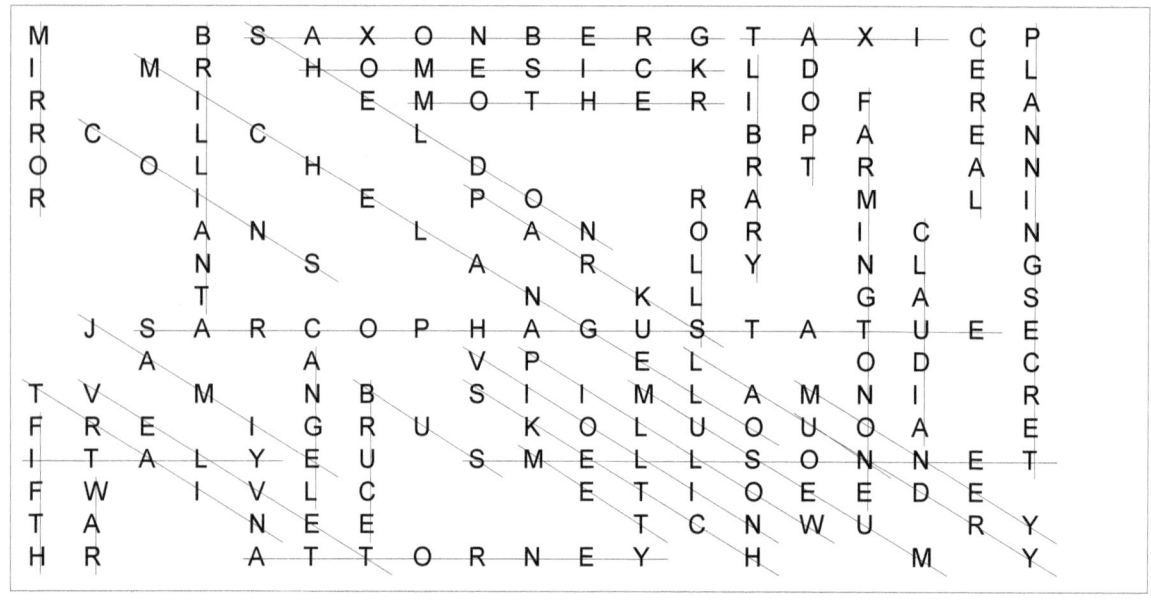

Angel left three rings with a W on this. (6)
Being away from home is not making Claudia and Jamie ____. (8)
Card game Jamie and Bruce play for money (3)
Claudia and Jamie run out of clean ____. (7)
Claudia and Jamie skip school by hiding in the school _____. (3)
Claudia and Jamie take a tour of the ____. (2)
Claudia and Mrs. Frankweiler both like keeping these. (6)
Claudia finds a _____ ticket in the wastebasket. (5)
Claudia places Jamie's instructions for running away here. (6)
Claudia sends for a rebate from this type of company. (6)
Claudia treasures good, clean ____. (6)
Claudia uses her ____ case as a suitcase. (6)
Claudia's special talent (8)
He created Angel. (12)
He makes extra money gambling at cards. (5)
He plays cards with Jamie on the school bus. (5)
How Claudia and Jamie travel to Farmington, Connecticut (4)
Impossible thing Mrs. Frankweiler would like to be (6)
Jamie flatters Claudia by calling her ____. (9)
Jamie is carrying $24.43 worth of these in his pockets. (5)
Jamie suggests fingerprinting this for clues. (6)
Mrs. Frankweiler asks Parks to bring her one. (6)

Mrs. Frankweiler plans to bequeath this to the children. (6)
Mrs. Frankweiler's butler (5)
Mrs. Frankweiler's driver (7)
Mrs. Frankweiler's lawyer (9)
Number of hours the kids have to find the secret (3)
Occupation of Claudia and Jamie's grandfather (8)
One was written on the back of a sketch of Angel. (6)
Place Claudia and Jamie go to research Michelangelo (7)
Place Claudia and Jamie run away to (6)
Place Claudia hides her violin case (11)
Playing cards and the fountain are sources of this. (5)
She plans to run away. (7)
Short for The Metropolitan Museum of Art (3)
Strolling down _____ Avenue may cause Claudia to shop. (5)
The children are driven home in a ____ Royce. (5)
The children plan to secretly _____ Mrs. Frankweiler. (5)
The secret answer was found in the Bologna, ____ file. (5)
The statue with a secret (5)
Town where Mrs. Frankweiler lives (10)

From the Mixed Up Files . . . Word Search 2

```
K O N I G S B U R G D I F F E R E N T P
B K B V P L A N N I N G C B Q Q D M H Y
C Z M I L D C M K R S B C E K B G I N N
S G H O M E S I C K O M W S R B V C K B
C H Y L N Q C C H M N X C A Y E T H Q B
J R O I C E S A X O N B E R G S A E L U
C O I N S Z Y M U S E U M C S M E L L S
C T P S E N N J D C T G X O H B N A S L
L P R F V S L A U N D R Y P E Z N N K Y
A T T O R N E Y J A M I E H L A N G E L
U L T U A H P C G P M W M A D B M E T K
D I I N Q D K F R H A A E G O R I L C Z
I B S T B M O T H E R R T U N T R O H V
A R W A A R D P S L T S K S N A R G R N
H A T I V L U R T R O L L S Y X O A T H
Q R Q N T Y Y C S T A T U E W I R F I W
Z Y F I F T H V E L V E T P I L L O W N
```

Angel left three rings with a W on this. (6)
Author of From The Mixed Up Files of Mrs. Basil E. Frankweiler (10)
Being away from home is not making Claudia and Jamie ____. (8)
Card game Jamie and Bruce play for money (3)
Claudia and Jamie run out of clean ____. (7)
Claudia and Jamie skip school by hiding in the school ____. (3)
Claudia and Jamie take a tour of the ____. (2)
Claudia and Mrs. Frankweiler both like keeping these. (6)
Claudia finds a_____ ticket in the wastebasket. (5)
Claudia places Jamie's instructions for running away here. (6)
Claudia sends for a rebate from this type of company. (6)
Claudia treasures good, clean ____. (6)
Claudia uses her ____ case as a suitcase. (6)
Claudia wanted to return home this way. (9)
Claudia's special talent (8)
He created Angel. (12)
He makes extra money gambling at cards. (5)
He plays cards with Jamie on the school bus. (5)
How Claudia and Jamie travel to Farmington, Connecticut (4)
Impossible thing Mrs. Frankweiler would like to be (6)
Jamie is carrying $24.43 worth of these in his pockets. (5)

Jamie suggests fingerprinting this for clues. (6)
Mrs. Frankweiler asks Parks to bring her one. (6)
Mrs. Frankweiler plans to bequeath this to the children. (6)
Mrs. Frankweiler's butler (5)
Mrs. Frankweiler's driver (7)
Mrs. Frankweiler's lawyer (9)
Number of hours the kids have to find the secret (3)
Occupation of Claudia and Jamie's grandfather (8)
One was written on the back of a sketch of Angel. (6)
Place Claudia and Jamie bathe (8)
Place Claudia and Jamie go to research Michelangelo (7)
Place Claudia and Jamie run away to (6)
Place Claudia hides her violin case (11)
Playing cards and the fountain are sources of this. (5)
She plans to run away. (7)
Short for The Metropolitan Museum of Art (3)
Strolling down _____ Avenue may cause Claudia to shop. (5)
The children are driven home in a ____ Royce. (5)
The children plan to secretly _____ Mrs. Frankweiler. (5)
The secret answer was found in the Bologna, ____ file. (5)
The statue with a secret (5)

From the Mixed Up Files... Word Search 2 Answer Key

Angel left three rings with a W on this. (6)
Author of From The Mixed Up Files of Mrs. Basil E. Frankweiler (10)
Being away from home is not making Claudia and Jamie ____. (8)
Card game Jamie and Bruce play for money (3)
Claudia and Jamie run out of clean ____. (7)
Claudia and Jamie skip school by hiding in the school ____. (3)
Claudia and Jamie take a tour of the ____. (2)
Claudia and Mrs. Frankweiler both like keeping these. (6)
Claudia finds a ____ ticket in the wastebasket. (5)
Claudia places Jamie's instructions for running away here. (6)
Claudia sends for a rebate from this type of company. (6)
Claudia treasures good, clean ____. (6)
Claudia uses her ____ case as a suitcase. (6)
Claudia wanted to return home this way. (9)
Claudia's special talent (8)
He created Angel. (12)
He makes extra money gambling at cards. (5)
He plays cards with Jamie on the school bus. (5)
How Claudia and Jamie travel to Farmington, Connecticut (4)
Impossible thing Mrs. Frankweiler would like to be (6)
Jamie is carrying $24.43 worth of these in his pockets. (5)

Jamie suggests fingerprinting this for clues. (6)
Mrs. Frankweiler asks Parks to bring her one. (6)
Mrs. Frankweiler plans to bequeath this to the children. (6)
Mrs. Frankweiler's butler (5)
Mrs. Frankweiler's driver (7)
Mrs. Frankweiler's lawyer (9)
Number of hours the kids have to find the secret (3)
Occupation of Claudia and Jamie's grandfather (8)
One was written on the back of a sketch of Angel. (6)
Place Claudia and Jamie bathe (8)
Place Claudia and Jamie go to research Michelangelo (7)
Place Claudia and Jamie run away to (6)
Place Claudia hides her violin case (11)
Playing cards and the fountain are sources of this. (5)
She plans to run away. (7)
Short for The Metropolitan Museum of Art (3)
Strolling down ____ Avenue may cause Claudia to shop. (5)
The children are driven home in a ____ Royce. (5)
The children plan to secretly ____ Mrs. Frankweiler. (5)
The secret answer was found in the Bologna, ____ file. (5)
The statue with a secret (5)

From the Mixed Up Files . . . Word Search 3

```
S N M B B S Z M A C F O U N T A I N L X
A A Z I T R G R O T P I F Z C S M J I Y
X C R Z R P I Y P T T G F L J E X N B W
O P L C V R Y L I J H O B T M C F J R M
N F X A O L O R L S R E R N H R R P A K
B R W L U P F R L I P L R N Q E Z L R Z
E A V Y A D H R O H A T R C E T S A Y T
R N Z L D D I A W X T N M F T Y J N X R
G K F J O Z G A G K F V T M D X A N V X
G W S D P Q P V Y U L W M P O Y M I N Z
C E L N T B W Y I C S R A A L N I N S M
D I F F E R E N T O N E B R U C E G O Q
M L B Z Q J A Z S G L R N K J L W Y N B
L E H O M E S I C K Y I Y S L A D Y N T
B R K F S B B Q N R D C N T D U D M E P
M U S E U M T J Z S H E L D O N X J T R
T C S Y I S E R X Y K R V C D D C G B B
B O L H X T F L S Z T E G H X R Q Q Q Y
J I M Q G W A L L A A T H C Y D K D C
A N G E L R O L L S X L U C V E L V E T
M S T A T U E D Y L I J N N H Q Y Q Y
```

ADOPT	FOUNTAIN	MUSEUM	SMELLS
ANGEL	FRANKWEILER	ONE	SONNET
ATTORNEY	HOMESICK	PARKS	STATUE
BRILLIANT	ITALY	PILLOW	TAXI
BRUCE	JAMIE	PLANNING	TRAIN
BUS	LAUNDRY	ROLLS	UN
CEREAL	LIBRARY	SARCOPHAGUS	VELVET
CLAUDIA	MET	SAXONBERG	VIOLIN
COINS	MIRROR	SECRET	WAR
DIFFERENT	MONEY	SHELDON	
FIFTH	MOTHER	SKETCH	

From the Mixed Up Files . . . Word Search 3 Answer Key

ADOPT	FOUNTAIN	MUSEUM	SMELLS
ANGEL	FRANKWEILER	ONE	SONNET
ATTORNEY	HOMESICK	PARKS	STATUE
BRILLIANT	ITALY	PILLOW	TAXI
BRUCE	JAMIE	PLANNING	TRAIN
BUS	LAUNDRY	ROLLS	UN
CEREAL	LIBRARY	SARCOPHAGUS	VELVET
CLAUDIA	MET	SAXONBERG	VIOLIN
COINS	MIRROR	SECRET	WAR
DIFFERENT	MONEY	SHELDON	
FIFTH	MOTHER	SKETCH	

From the Mixed Up Files . . . Word Search 4

```
S S C M I R R O R H M P A R K S F P H V
T O O E F R G D T K A O C G Z C R L O M
A N I T O A O H B T D C T X T P A A M G
T N N J U T R L K S O V C H S H N N E D
U E S A N T D M L B P M E K E S K N S C
E T F M T O W D I S T V R V J R W I I C
W H S I A R W S L N N Q E I D R E N C R
Z M A E I N X S A K G F A O C W I G K C
H I R C N E T G U O Y T L L W C L R Y S
M C C H C Y S L N N H C O I V A E L H W
D H O M M Y E Q D I Z F S N D T R A I N
C E P P O H C B R G T V M X Y T D Z B R
M L H C P N R W Y S L X E T S A K Q H C
F A A M U S E U M B R I L L I A N T C G
I N G U K F T Y D U U F L S Z T D G W G
F G U P D G M B G R O S S S K M A S E R
T E S I D I Q R J G N Y Q C S E Q L R L
H L W L Z V A U N V E L V E T L T W Y L
R O W L W K Z C L I B R A R Y F A C P V
J Z N O J S H E L D O N S J R S X W H J
B F D W D I F F E R E N T B Y Q I P F B
```

ADOPT	FIFTH	MIRROR	SHELDON
ANGEL	FOUNTAIN	MONEY	SKETCH
ATTORNEY	FRANKWEILER	MOTHER	SMELLS
BRILLIANT	HOMESICK	MUSEUM	SONNET
BRUCE	ITALY	ONE	STATUE
BUS	JAMIE	PARKS	TAXI
CEREAL	KONIGSBURG	PILLOW	TRAIN
CLAUDIA	LAUNDRY	PLANNING	UN
COINS	LIBRARY	ROLLS	VELVET
DIFFERENT	MET	SARCOPHAGUS	VIOLIN
FARMINGTON	MICHELANGELO	SECRET	WAR

From the Mixed Up Files . . . Word Search 4 Answer Key

```
S   S   C   M   I   R   R   O   R       M   P   A   R   K   S   F   P   H
T   O   O   E   F   R               A   O           R   L   O
A   N   I   T   O   A           D       T   C       A   A   M
T   N   J   J   U   T   R       O       C       H   N   N   E
U   E   S   A   N   T       M   P       E       E   K   N   S
E   T       M   T   O               T   R   I       W   I   I
        S   I   A   R           L       E   O       E   N   C
        A   E   I   N       L   A       A       W   I   G   K
    M   R       N   E       A   U       L       A   L
    I   C           Y   S   U   N   G   O   T   T   E
    C   O           M   E   N   D           S       R   A   I   N
    H   P       O       C   D   I           M       A
    E   H       N       R   R   G           E       N
C   L   A   M   U   S   E   U   M   B   R   I   L   L   I   A   N   T
F   A   N   U       T       Y   U       L       S   K       T   G
I   N   G   P       D       B   R       O   S       K       A   E
F   G   U   I           A   R   G           N           E   L   L
T   E   S   L               A   U   N   V   E   L   V   E   T
H   L       L               C   L   I   B   R   A   R   Y   T   C
    O       O       S   H   E   L   D   O   N               A   H
            W   D   I   F   F   E   R   E   N   T           X
                                                            I
```

ADOPT	FIFTH	MIRROR	SHELDON
ANGEL	FOUNTAIN	MONEY	SKETCH
ATTORNEY	FRANKWEILER	MOTHER	SMELLS
BRILLIANT	HOMESICK	MUSEUM	SONNET
BRUCE	ITALY	ONE	STATUE
BUS	JAMIE	PARKS	TAXI
CEREAL	KONIGSBURG	PILLOW	TRAIN
CLAUDIA	LAUNDRY	PLANNING	UN
COINS	LIBRARY	ROLLS	VELVET
DIFFERENT	MET	SARCOPHAGUS	VIOLIN
FARMINGTON	MICHELANGELO	SECRET	WAR

From the Mixed Up Files . . . Crossword 1

Across
1. He created Angel.
7. The children are driven home in a ____ Royce.
8. Claudia and Jamie skip school by hiding in the school _____.
9. Card game Jamie and Bruce play for money
10. Claudia and Jamie take a tour of the ____.
11. He plays cards with Jamie on the school bus.
13. Place Claudia and Jamie bathe
15. How Claudia and Jamie travel to Farmington, Connecticut
18. Jamie suggests fingerprinting this for clues.
19. Claudia places Jamie's instructions for running away here.
20. Mrs. Frankweiler's butler
21. Short for The Metropolitan Museum of Art
22. He makes extra money gambling at cards.

Down
1. Place Claudia and Jamie run away to
2. Claudia sends for a rebate from this type of company.
3. Claudia and Jamie run out of clean ____.
4. Place Claudia and Jamie go to research Michelangelo
5. Claudia finds a _____ ticket in the wastebasket.
6. Claudia's special talent
12. She plans to run away.
13. Strolling down _____ Avenue may cause Claudia to shop.
14. Occupation of Claudia and Jamie's grandfather
16. The secret answer was found in the Bologna, ____ file.
17. Angel left three rings with a W on this.

From the Mixed Up Files . . . Crossword 1 Answer Key

```
                    1 M  I  C  H  2 E  L  A  3 N  G  E  4 L  O
              5 T      6 P     U        E        A           I
              7 R  O   L  L    S        8 B  U   S           B
                 A     A       E           U              9 W A R
                 I     N       U           N           W
           10 U  N     N       M        11 B  R   U  12 C  E  R
                       I                   Y            L      Y
           13 F  O  U  N  T 14 A  I  N              15 T A 16 X  I
              I           G   T                17 V    U      T
              F        18 S   A  T  U    E        E    D      A
              T           O                        L 19 P  I  L  L  O W
              H        20 P   A  R  K    S         V    A     Y
                          N              21 M  E   T
                       22 J   A  M  I    E
                              Y
```

Across
1. He created Angel.
7. The children are driven home in a ____ Royce.
8. Claudia and Jamie skip school by hiding in the school _____.
9. Card game Jamie and Bruce play for money
10. Claudia and Jamie take a tour of the ____.
11. He plays cards with Jamie on the school bus.
13. Place Claudia and Jamie bathe
15. How Claudia and Jamie travel to Farmington, Connecticut
18. Jamie suggests fingerprinting this for clues.
19. Claudia places Jamie's instructions for running away here.
20. Mrs. Frankweiler's butler
21. Short for The Metropolitan Museum of Art
22. He makes extra money gambling at cards.

Down
1. Place Claudia and Jamie run away to
2. Claudia sends for a rebate from this type of company.
3. Claudia and Jamie run out of clean ____.
4. Place Claudia and Jamie go to research Michelangelo
5. Claudia finds a _____ ticket in the wastebasket.
6. Claudia's special talent
12. She plans to run away.
13. Strolling down _____ Avenue may cause Claudia to shop.
14. Occupation of Claudia and Jamie's grandfather
16. The secret answer was found in the Bologna, ____ file.
17. Angel left three rings with a W on this.

From the Mixed Up Files . . . Crossword 2

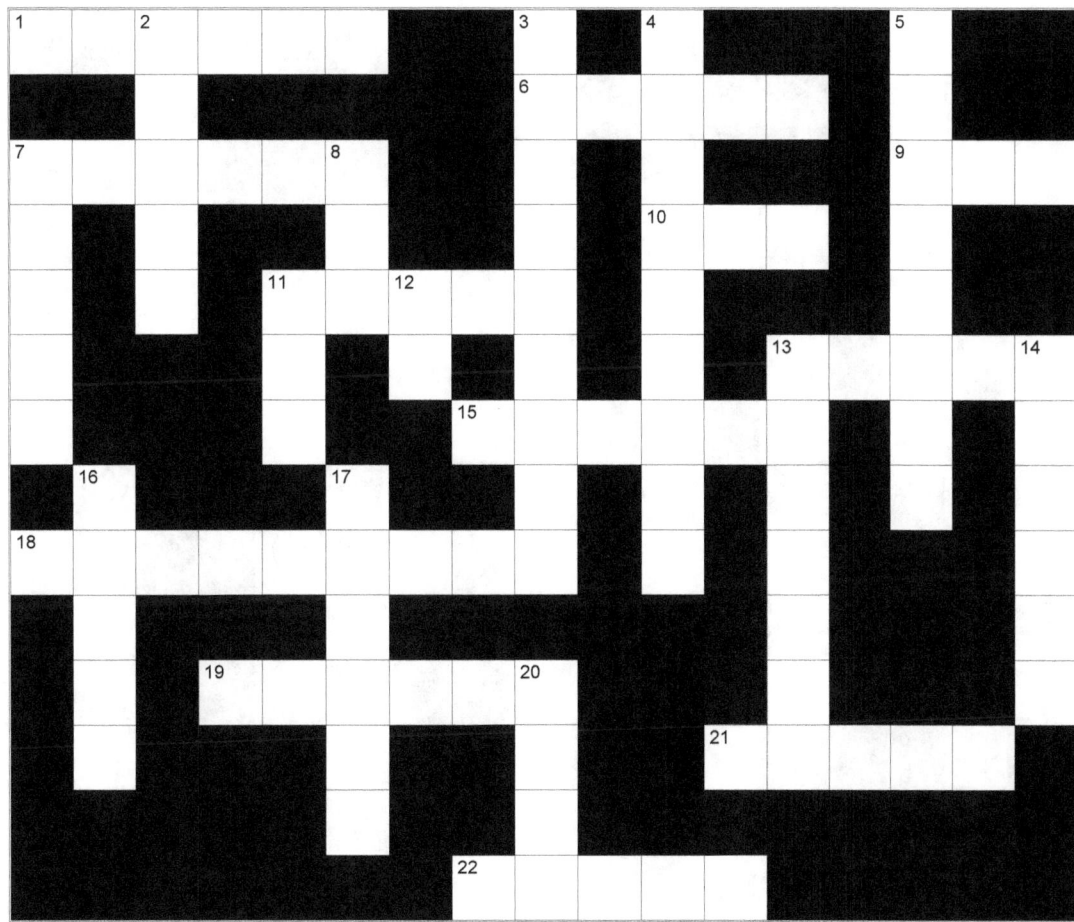

Across
1. Mrs. Frankweiler asks Parks to bring her one.
6. The secret answer was found in the Bologna, ____ file.
7. Claudia places Jamie's instructions for running away here.
9. Short for The Metropolitan Museum of Art
10. Number of hours the kids have to find the secret
11. He plays cards with Jamie on the school bus.
13. Jamie is carrying $24.43 worth of these in his pockets.
15. Claudia sends for a rebate from this type of company.
18. Jamie flatters Claudia by calling her ____.
19. Angel left three rings with a W on this.
21. He makes extra money gambling at cards.
22. Strolling down _____ Avenue may cause Claudia to shop.

Down
2. The children are driven home in a ____ Royce.
3. Claudia wanted to return home this way.
4. Mrs. Frankweiler's lawyer
5. Being away from home is not making Claudia and Jamie ____.
7. Mrs. Frankweiler's butler
8. Card game Jamie and Bruce play for money
11. Claudia and Jamie skip school by hiding in the school _____.
12. Claudia and Jamie take a tour of the ____.
13. She plans to run away.
14. Claudia and Mrs. Frankweiler both like keeping these.
16. Claudia finds a_____ ticket in the wastebasket.
17. Claudia uses her ____ case as a suitcase.
20. How Claudia and Jamie travel to Farmington, Connecticut

From the Mixed Up Files . . . Crossword 2 Answer Key

	1 M	I	2 R	R	O	R			3 D		4 S				5 H	
			O						6 I	T	A	L	Y		O	
	7 P	I	L	L	O	W		8 W		F	X				9 M	E	T
	A					A				F	10 O	N	E		E	
	R		L	S		11 B	R	12 U	C	E		N			S	
	K					U		N		R		B		13 C	O	I	N	14 S
	S					S			15 C	E	R	E	A	L		C		E
		16 T					17 V		E		N		R		A		K		C
	18 B	R	I	L	L	I	A	N	T		R		G		U		R
		A					O				D						E
		I		19 V	E	L	V	E	T		20 T						T
		N					I		A		21 J	A	M	I	E
							N		X						
									22 F	I	F	T	H		

Across
1. Mrs. Frankweiler asks Parks to bring her one.
6. The secret answer was found in the Bologna, ____ file.
7. Claudia places Jamie's instructions for running away here.
9. Short for The Metropolitan Museum of Art
10. Number of hours the kids have to find the secret
11. He plays cards with Jamie on the school bus.
13. Jamie is carrying $24.43 worth of these in his pockets.
15. Claudia sends for a rebate from this type of company.
18. Jamie flatters Claudia by calling her ____.
19. Angel left three rings with a W on this.
21. He makes extra money gambling at cards.
22. Strolling down ____ Avenue may cause Claudia to shop.

Down
2. The children are driven home in a ____ Royce.
3. Claudia wanted to return home this way.
4. Mrs. Frankweiler's lawyer
5. Being away from home is not making Claudia and Jamie ____.
7. Mrs. Frankweiler's butler
8. Card game Jamie and Bruce play for money
11. Claudia and Jamie skip school by hiding in the school ____.
12. Claudia and Jamie take a tour of the ____.
13. She plans to run away.
14. Claudia and Mrs. Frankweiler both like keeping these.
16. Claudia finds a_____ ticket in the wastebasket.
17. Claudia uses her ____ case as a suitcase.
20. How Claudia and Jamie travel to Farmington, Connecticut

From the Mixed Up Files . . . Crossword 3

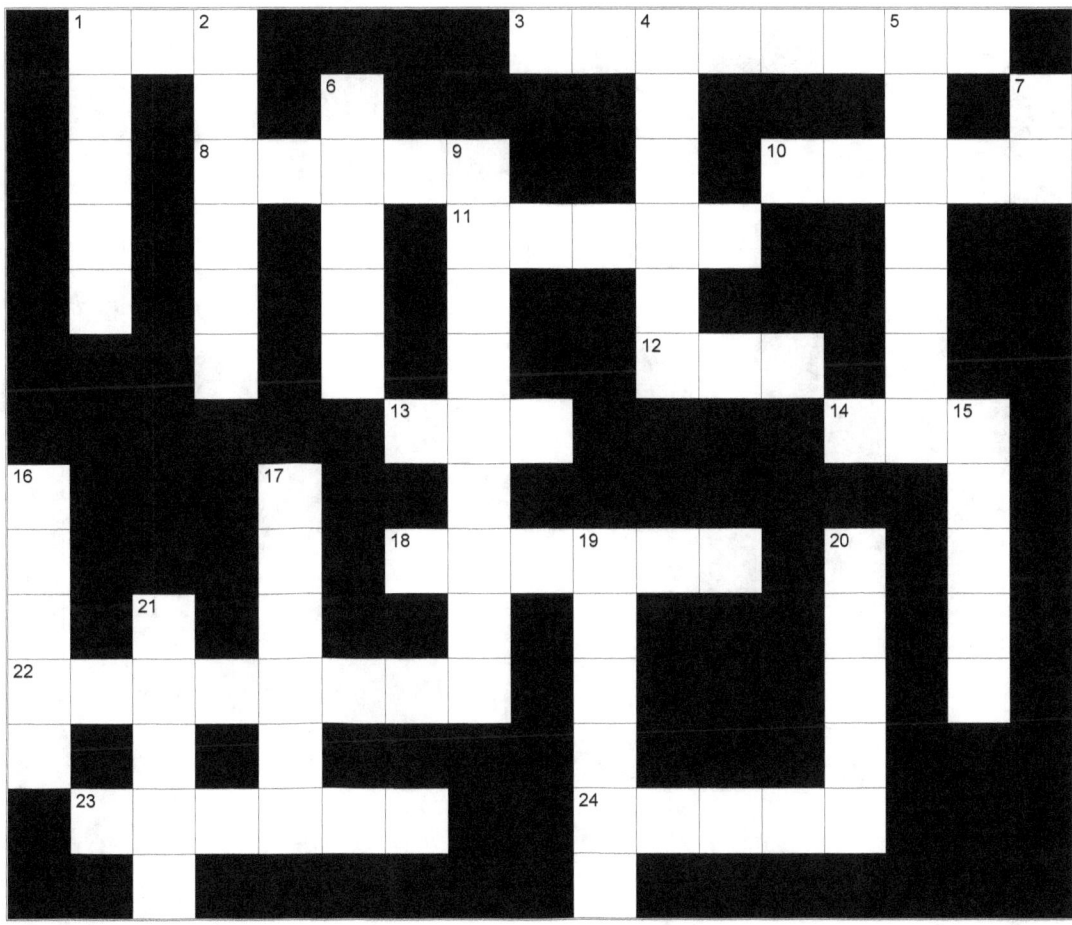

Across
1. Claudia and Jamie skip school by hiding in the school _____.
3. Being away from home is not making Claudia and Jamie ____.
8. Jamie is carrying $24.43 worth of these in his pockets.
10. Claudia finds a _____ ticket in the wastebasket.
11. The statue with a secret
12. Short for The Metropolitan Museum of Art
13. Number of hours the kids have to find the secret
14. Card game Jamie and Bruce play for money
18. Angel left three rings with a W on this.
22. Claudia's special talent
23. Mrs. Frankweiler plans to bequeath this to the children.
24. The secret answer was found in the Bologna, ____ file.

Down
1. He plays cards with Jamie on the school bus.
2. Claudia and Mrs. Frankweiler both like keeping these.
4. Place Claudia and Jamie run away to
5. She plans to run away.
6. Strolling down _____ Avenue may cause Claudia to shop.
7. Claudia and Jamie take a tour of the ____.
9. Mrs. Frankweiler's lawyer
15. The children are driven home in a ____ Royce.
16. The children plan to secretly _____ Mrs. Frankweiler.
17. One was written on the back of a sketch of Angel.
19. Claudia uses her ____ case as a suitcase.
20. Playing cards and the fountain are sources of this.
21. Mrs. Frankweiler's butler

From the Mixed Up Files . . . Crossword 3 Answer Key

Across
1. Claudia and Jamie skip school by hiding in the school _____.
3. Being away from home is not making Claudia and Jamie ____.
8. Jamie is carrying $24.43 worth of these in his pockets.
10. Claudia finds a _____ ticket in the wastebasket.
11. The statue with a secret
12. Short for The Metropolitan Museum of Art
13. Number of hours the kids have to find the secret
14. Card game Jamie and Bruce play for money
18. Angel left three rings with a W on this.
22. Claudia's special talent
23. Mrs. Frankweiler plans to bequeath this to the children.
24. The secret answer was found in the Bologna, ____ file.

Down
1. He plays cards with Jamie on the school bus.
2. Claudia and Mrs. Frankweiler both like keeping these.
4. Place Claudia and Jamie run away to
5. She plans to run away.
6. Strolling down _____ Avenue may cause Claudia to shop.
7. Claudia and Jamie take a tour of the ____.
9. Mrs. Frankweiler's lawyer
15. The children are driven home in a ____ Royce.
16. The children plan to secretly _____ Mrs. Frankweiler.
17. One was written on the back of a sketch of Angel.
19. Claudia uses her ____ case as a suitcase.
20. Playing cards and the fountain are sources of this.
21. Mrs. Frankweiler's butler

From the Mixed Up Files . . . Crossword 4

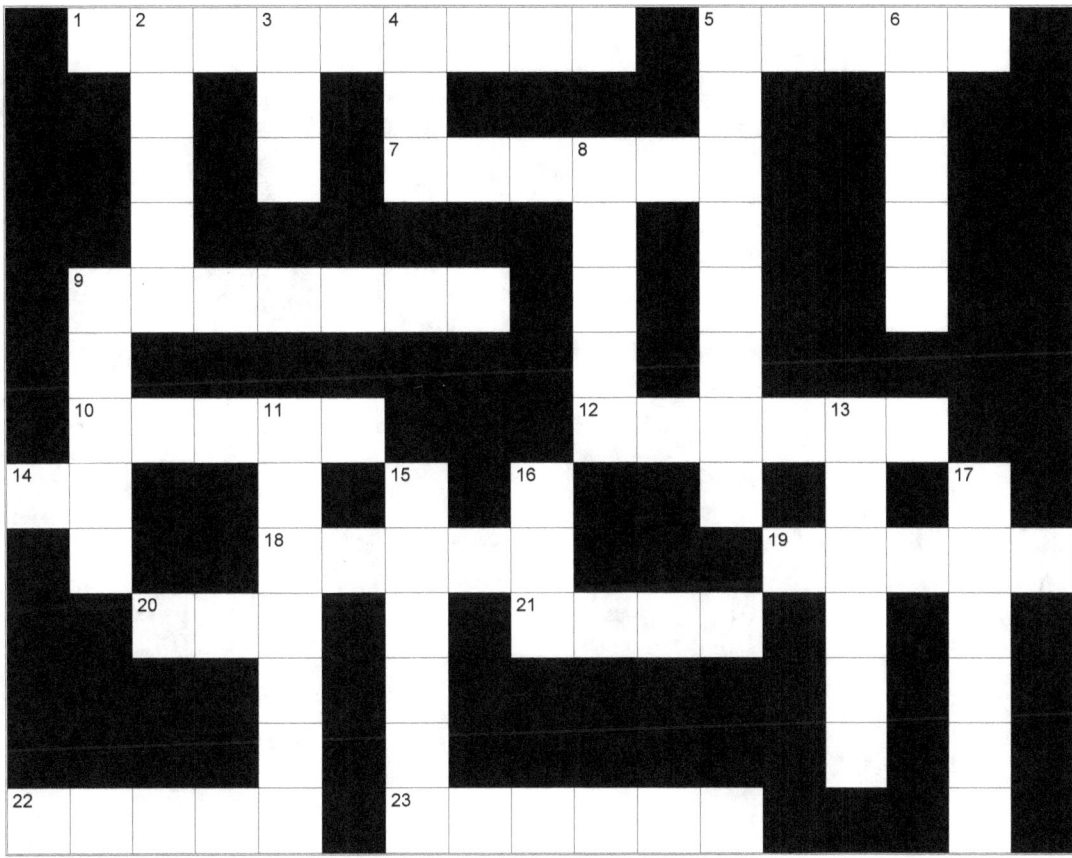

Across
1. Mrs. Frankweiler's lawyer
5. The children plan to secretly _____ Mrs. Frankweiler.
7. Claudia and Mrs. Frankweiler both like keeping these.
9. She plans to run away.
10. The secret answer was found in the Bologna, ____ file.
12. Mrs. Frankweiler plans to bequeath this to the children.
14. Claudia and Jamie take a tour of the ____.
18. He plays cards with Jamie on the school bus.
19. Claudia finds a _____ ticket in the wastebasket.
20. Card game Jamie and Bruce play for money
21. How Claudia and Jamie travel to Farmington, Connecticut
22. Playing cards and the fountain are sources of this.
23. Mrs. Frankweiler asks Parks to bring her one.

Down
2. The statue with a secret
3. Number of hours the kids have to find the secret
4. Claudia and Jamie skip school by hiding in the school _____.
5. Occupation of Claudia and Jamie's grandfather
6. Mrs. Frankweiler's butler
8. The children are driven home in a ____ Royce.
9. Jamie is carrying $24.43 worth of these in his pockets.
11. Place Claudia and Jamie go to research Michelangelo
13. Claudia sends for a rebate from this type of company.
15. Place Claudia and Jamie run away to
16. Short for The Metropolitan Museum of Art
17. Claudia uses her ____ case as a suitcase.

From the Mixed Up Files . . . Crossword 4 Answer Key

	1 S	2 A	3 X	4 O	N	B	E	R	G		5 A	D	6 O	P	T
		N		N		U					T		A		
		G		E		7 S	E	8 C	R	E	T		R		
		E						O			O		K		
	9 C	L	A	U	D	I	A		L		R		S		
	O								L		N				
	10 I	T	A	11 L	Y			12 S	K	E	T	13 C	H		
14 U	N			I		15 M		16 M			Y		E		17 V
	S			18 B	R	U	C	E				19 T	R	A	I	N
			20 W	A	R	S		21 T	A	X	I		E		O
						A		E					A		L
						R		U					L		I
	22 M	O	N	E	Y			23 M	I	R	R	O	R		N

Across
1. Mrs. Frankweiler's lawyer
5. The children plan to secretly _____ Mrs. Frankweiler.
7. Claudia and Mrs. Frankweiler both like keeping these.
9. She plans to run away.
10. The secret answer was found in the Bologna, ____ file.
12. Mrs. Frankweiler plans to bequeath this to the children.
14. Claudia and Jamie take a tour of the ____.
18. He plays cards with Jamie on the school bus.
19. Claudia finds a _____ ticket in the wastebasket.
20. Card game Jamie and Bruce play for money
21. How Claudia and Jamie travel to Farmington, Connecticut
22. Playing cards and the fountain are sources of this.
23. Mrs. Frankweiler asks Parks to bring her one.

Down
2. The statue with a secret
3. Number of hours the kids have to find the secret
4. Claudia and Jamie skip school by hiding in the school _____.
5. Occupation of Claudia and Jamie's grandfather
6. Mrs. Frankweiler's butler
8. The children are driven home in a ____ Royce.
9. Jamie is carrying $24.43 worth of these in his pockets.
11. Place Claudia and Jamie go to research Michelangelo
13. Claudia sends for a rebate from this type of company.
15. Place Claudia and Jamie run away to
16. Short for The Metropolitan Museum of Art
17. Claudia uses her ____ case as a suitcase.

From the Mixed Up Files . . .

LIBRARY	BUS	SAXONBERG	MOTHER	ITALY
MIRROR	SONNET	HOMESICK	KONIGSBURG	TAXI
FRANKWEILER	JAMIE	FREE SPACE	PILLOW	LAUNDRY
SECRET	CEREAL	ADOPT	COINS	MONEY
PARKS	BRUCE	SARCOPHAGUS	MUSEUM	DIFFERENT

From the Mixed Up Files . . .

VIOLIN	CLAUDIA	SHELDON	MICHELANGELO	SKETCH
FIFTH	UN	ATTORNEY	WAR	TRAIN
ONE	FOUNTAIN	FREE SPACE	ANGEL	SMELLS
FARMINGTON	PLANNING	BRILLIANT	ROLLS	MET
DIFFERENT	MUSEUM	SARCOPHAGUS	BRUCE	PARKS

From the Mixed Up Files . . .

ATTORNEY	SONNET	BRILLIANT	UN	MET
TRAIN	CLAUDIA	LAUNDRY	FARMINGTON	KONIGSBURG
VELVET	PLANNING	FREE SPACE	SAXONBERG	COINS
HOMESICK	SMELLS	PILLOW	FIFTH	SARCOPHAGUS
SHELDON	MOTHER	STATUE	MIRROR	SECRET

From the Mixed Up Files . . .

ADOPT	PARKS	FRANKWEILER	TAXI	WAR
ITALY	DIFFERENT	FOUNTAIN	ROLLS	BUS
LIBRARY	ANGEL	FREE SPACE	VIOLIN	MUSEUM
BRUCE	JAMIE	CEREAL	SKETCH	ONE
SECRET	MIRROR	STATUE	MOTHER	SHELDON

From the Mixed Up Files . . .

ATTORNEY	MIRROR	TRAIN	PLANNING	SARCOPHAGUS
JAMIE	FRANKWEILER	BRILLIANT	FIFTH	FOUNTAIN
UN	FARMINGTON	FREE SPACE	DIFFERENT	ANGEL
VELVET	ROLLS	KONIGSBURG	MET	SHELDON
ADOPT	MONEY	STATUE	LIBRARY	COINS

From the Mixed Up Files . . .

SMELLS	WAR	SKETCH	SECRET	BRUCE
BUS	PARKS	MOTHER	PILLOW	LAUNDRY
TAXI	HOMESICK	FREE SPACE	MUSEUM	ONE
SONNET	SAXONBERG	ITALY	CLAUDIA	MICHELANGELO
COINS	LIBRARY	STATUE	MONEY	ADOPT

From the Mixed Up Files . . .

SONNET	ANGEL	LAUNDRY	UN	STATUE
VIOLIN	FARMINGTON	MONEY	BUS	MET
CLAUDIA	CEREAL	FREE SPACE	PLANNING	MICHELANGELO
SAXONBERG	BRILLIANT	LIBRARY	SHELDON	ADOPT
VELVET	JAMIE	COINS	SECRET	FRANKWEILER

From the Mixed Up Files . . .

WAR	PILLOW	ATTORNEY	SMELLS	ITALY
FOUNTAIN	TAXI	KONIGSBURG	BRUCE	MOTHER
MIRROR	MUSEUM	FREE SPACE	DIFFERENT	HOMESICK
ONE	SARCOPHAGUS	SKETCH	ROLLS	FIFTH
FRANKWEILER	SECRET	COINS	JAMIE	VELVET

From the Mixed Up Files . . .

SAXONBERG	VELVET	LIBRARY	TRAIN	JAMIE
LAUNDRY	BRUCE	TAXI	SMELLS	FARMINGTON
MIRROR	FRANKWEILER	FREE SPACE	PARKS	STATUE
MICHELANGELO	ANGEL	VIOLIN	COINS	ROLLS
HOMESICK	MOTHER	SHELDON	ATTORNEY	ONE

From the Mixed Up Files . . .

CEREAL	FIFTH	WAR	KONIGSBURG	MUSEUM
ITALY	SKETCH	FOUNTAIN	SARCOPHAGUS	DIFFERENT
MONEY	PLANNING	FREE SPACE	MET	UN
CLAUDIA	BUS	ADOPT	PILLOW	SECRET
ONE	ATTORNEY	SHELDON	MOTHER	HOMESICK

From the Mixed Up Files . . .

KONIGSBURG	COINS	ONE	FOUNTAIN	SKETCH
MOTHER	SONNET	VIOLIN	MICHELANGELO	PLANNING
ADOPT	PILLOW	FREE SPACE	ITALY	SAXONBERG
SMELLS	WAR	FRANKWEILER	ROLLS	MONEY
FARMINGTON	BUS	MUSEUM	SARCOPHAGUS	STATUE

From the Mixed Up Files . . .

PARKS	SECRET	MIRROR	ATTORNEY	DIFFERENT
BRILLIANT	CEREAL	JAMIE	LIBRARY	FIFTH
BRUCE	UN	FREE SPACE	TAXI	VELVET
MET	CLAUDIA	ANGEL	LAUNDRY	TRAIN
STATUE	SARCOPHAGUS	MUSEUM	BUS	FARMINGTON

From the Mixed Up Files . . .

CEREAL	SECRET	CLAUDIA	MICHELANGELO	BUS
MIRROR	FIFTH	SAXONBERG	MONEY	TRAIN
JAMIE	VIOLIN	FREE SPACE	FARMINGTON	TAXI
FOUNTAIN	PILLOW	SHELDON	ITALY	MOTHER
DIFFERENT	SARCOPHAGUS	LIBRARY	WAR	BRUCE

From the Mixed Up Files . . .

KONIGSBURG	VELVET	ADOPT	PARKS	LAUNDRY
ATTORNEY	MET	PLANNING	STATUE	FRANKWEILER
SKETCH	COINS	FREE SPACE	HOMESICK	SMELLS
ROLLS	UN	ANGEL	SONNET	MUSEUM
BRUCE	WAR	LIBRARY	SARCOPHAGUS	DIFFERENT

From the Mixed Up Files . . .

DIFFERENT	SMELLS	TRAIN	VIOLIN	SHELDON
SKETCH	FARMINGTON	BUS	SARCOPHAGUS	STATUE
MET	TAXI	FREE SPACE	ROLLS	BRILLIANT
LAUNDRY	BRUCE	ADOPT	VELVET	KONIGSBURG
PLANNING	FRANKWEILER	PILLOW	MONEY	CEREAL

From the Mixed Up Files . . .

SONNET	ITALY	SECRET	MICHELANGELO	PARKS
LIBRARY	COINS	HOMESICK	FIFTH	MOTHER
FOUNTAIN	ATTORNEY	FREE SPACE	JAMIE	MUSEUM
SAXONBERG	MIRROR	UN	ANGEL	WAR
CEREAL	MONEY	PILLOW	FRANKWEILER	PLANNING

From the Mixed Up Files . . .

MOTHER	PARKS	SAXONBERG	CEREAL	FARMINGTON
JAMIE	KONIGSBURG	TAXI	ANGEL	HOMESICK
WAR	BRILLIANT	FREE SPACE	SHELDON	ADOPT
SMELLS	MUSEUM	MONEY	COINS	MET
LAUNDRY	SONNET	ITALY	FIFTH	ROLLS

From the Mixed Up Files . . .

BRUCE	TRAIN	BUS	DIFFERENT	FOUNTAIN
PILLOW	LIBRARY	STATUE	VELVET	MIRROR
SKETCH	PLANNING	FREE SPACE	FRANKWEILER	UN
ONE	ATTORNEY	SECRET	VIOLIN	SARCOPHAGUS
ROLLS	FIFTH	ITALY	SONNET	LAUNDRY

From the Mixed Up Files . . .

SAXONBERG	FARMINGTON	VIOLIN	HOMESICK	JAMIE
BRUCE	LIBRARY	CEREAL	PILLOW	ITALY
UN	LAUNDRY	FREE SPACE	BUS	PARKS
STATUE	MIRROR	MET	TRAIN	SKETCH
SECRET	SARCOPHAGUS	BRILLIANT	CLAUDIA	ATTORNEY

From the Mixed Up Files . . .

FOUNTAIN	MICHELANGELO	ONE	SMELLS	MONEY
SONNET	ANGEL	MOTHER	PLANNING	FIFTH
ROLLS	WAR	FREE SPACE	COINS	TAXI
MUSEUM	SHELDON	ADOPT	KONIGSBURG	VELVET
ATTORNEY	CLAUDIA	BRILLIANT	SARCOPHAGUS	SECRET

From the Mixed Up Files . . .

BUS	TAXI	VELVET	JAMIE	PARKS
FRANKWEILER	ATTORNEY	CLAUDIA	BRILLIANT	SAXONBERG
FIFTH	LAUNDRY	FREE SPACE	SARCOPHAGUS	COINS
SONNET	HOMESICK	MET	ITALY	MICHELANGELO
MUSEUM	ROLLS	BRUCE	KONIGSBURG	MOTHER

From the Mixed Up Files . . .

SKETCH	LIBRARY	FOUNTAIN	SMELLS	ONE
DIFFERENT	PILLOW	FARMINGTON	MIRROR	CEREAL
WAR	SHELDON	FREE SPACE	ANGEL	MONEY
STATUE	TRAIN	ADOPT	PLANNING	SECRET
MOTHER	KONIGSBURG	BRUCE	ROLLS	MUSEUM

From the Mixed Up Files . . .

CEREAL	BUS	ROLLS	STATUE	LAUNDRY
MET	VIOLIN	TRAIN	PLANNING	FOUNTAIN
KONIGSBURG	LIBRARY	FREE SPACE	FRANKWEILER	ONE
FARMINGTON	MUSEUM	PILLOW	UN	JAMIE
SAXONBERG	COINS	FIFTH	CLAUDIA	BRILLIANT

From the Mixed Up Files . . .

SMELLS	ANGEL	WAR	HOMESICK	PARKS
SONNET	BRUCE	VELVET	MONEY	ADOPT
SHELDON	DIFFERENT	FREE SPACE	MICHELANGELO	SARCOPHAGUS
ITALY	ATTORNEY	SECRET	MIRROR	MOTHER
BRILLIANT	CLAUDIA	FIFTH	COINS	SAXONBERG

From the Mixed Up Files . . .

PARKS	ONE	SONNET	VELVET	KONIGSBURG
MOTHER	HOMESICK	SECRET	VIOLIN	MUSEUM
MIRROR	BUS	FREE SPACE	ITALY	SHELDON
BRILLIANT	SMELLS	UN	STATUE	FIFTH
FRANKWEILER	COINS	DIFFERENT	CEREAL	SKETCH

From the Mixed Up Files . . .

LIBRARY	MONEY	ATTORNEY	PLANNING	TAXI
TRAIN	CLAUDIA	MICHELANGELO	FARMINGTON	ANGEL
SARCOPHAGUS	MET	FREE SPACE	LAUNDRY	SAXONBERG
ROLLS	FOUNTAIN	ADOPT	PILLOW	BRUCE
SKETCH	CEREAL	DIFFERENT	COINS	FRANKWEILER

From the Mixed Up Files . . .

SONNET	TAXI	COINS	VELVET	VIOLIN
FIFTH	TRAIN	PLANNING	MOTHER	CEREAL
FOUNTAIN	SHELDON	FREE SPACE	UN	MIRROR
BUS	MICHELANGELO	BRILLIANT	ROLLS	SARCOPHAGUS
FARMINGTON	MUSEUM	CLAUDIA	BRUCE	PARKS

From the Mixed Up Files . . .

HOMESICK	LAUNDRY	ITALY	SKETCH	PILLOW
SECRET	MET	JAMIE	MONEY	FRANKWEILER
DIFFERENT	ATTORNEY	FREE SPACE	KONIGSBURG	SMELLS
ADOPT	WAR	ONE	SAXONBERG	STATUE
PARKS	BRUCE	CLAUDIA	MUSEUM	FARMINGTON

From the Mixed Up Files . . .

MET	LAUNDRY	BRUCE	SARCOPHAGUS	VELVET
STATUE	TAXI	MICHELANGELO	SMELLS	VIOLIN
CEREAL	ITALY	FREE SPACE	MOTHER	SKETCH
KONIGSBURG	FIFTH	FOUNTAIN	ATTORNEY	PARKS
TRAIN	HOMESICK	LIBRARY	ROLLS	CLAUDIA

From the Mixed Up Files . . .

ANGEL	PLANNING	MIRROR	JAMIE	MUSEUM
SECRET	ADOPT	SAXONBERG	MONEY	BUS
BRILLIANT	SHELDON	FREE SPACE	FRANKWEILER	UN
PILLOW	WAR	COINS	DIFFERENT	SONNET
CLAUDIA	ROLLS	LIBRARY	HOMESICK	TRAIN

From the Mixed Up Files . . .

ONE	MET	COINS	VELVET	BRUCE
MUSEUM	MONEY	DIFFERENT	ANGEL	FARMINGTON
TAXI	SECRET	FREE SPACE	KONIGSBURG	BUS
ADOPT	PLANNING	SHELDON	LIBRARY	SMELLS
SONNET	FIFTH	STATUE	PARKS	HOMESICK

From the Mixed Up Files . . .

SAXONBERG	SKETCH	PILLOW	ROLLS	JAMIE
VIOLIN	TRAIN	LAUNDRY	CEREAL	FOUNTAIN
MOTHER	MIRROR	FREE SPACE	WAR	UN
SARCOPHAGUS	ATTORNEY	ITALY	BRILLIANT	CLAUDIA
HOMESICK	PARKS	STATUE	FIFTH	SONNET

Mixed-Up Files Vocabulary Word List

No.	Word	Clue/Definition
1.	ABRASIONS	Areas of the skin that has been hurt by scraping
2.	ACCURATE	Precise and correct
3.	ACCUSTOMED	Become used to a certain thing or way of doing things
4.	ADVISED	Recommended
5.	ALLOTTED	Gave something to somebody as his or her share of what is available
6.	AMASSED	Collected over time until they form a large fund
7.	ASCENDED	Went upward
8.	ASSOCIATED	Connected to or having to do with
9.	ATTRIBUTING	Giving credit to a person for a particular piece of art or work of literature
10.	BAROQUE	An ornamental style of European art (mid-16th to early 18th centuries)
11.	BROWSING	Looking around in a leisurely manner
12.	CAPER	A light-hearted adventure or a dangerous illegal activity
13.	CHAUFFEUR	Driver
14.	CLAMPED	Held tightly over
15.	COMMOTION	Noisy activity or confusion
16.	COMPLEMENTED	Something completed something else, or made it close to perfect
17.	COUNTERED	To say something that contradicts what someone else has said
18.	COUNTERFEITED	Made a realistic copy of
19.	DECEASED	Dead
20.	DELINQUENT	A young person who has broken the law
21.	DESCENDING	Coming down
22.	DIRECTED	Pointed someone in a particular direction
23.	DISCLOSING	Revealing or telling about
24.	DISMALLY	In a depressing manner
25.	DISMISS	To officially release students from school
26.	DRIZZLE	To rain lightly
27.	EMERGE	To appear
28.	EXPOSED	Revealed
29.	FLATTERY	The act of complimenting someone for the purpose of getting something
30.	FOOTNOTES	An explanation at the bottom of a page giving further information about something in the text above
31.	HODGEPODGE	A mixture of several unrelated things
32.	HUMILITY	A feeling of modesty
33.	IMPOSTER	Someone who pretends to be someone he is not
34.	INJUSTICE	Unfair treatment
35.	INTRIGUED	To make someone very interested
36.	KEEN	Slang term for very cool
37.	LIBERTY	Freedom to think or act
38.	MAIMED	Affected with a severe and permanent injury
39.	MASTABA	An ancient Egyptian tomb with a flat base, sloping sides, and a flat roof
40.	MATINEE	An afternoon performance of a play, usually with cheaper seats than the evening performance
41.	MEDIOCRE	Adequate, but not very good
42.	MONOTONY	boredom that comes from doing the same thing over and over
43.	MUMMIES	Bodies of people that have been embalmed and wrapped in cloth, as was the custom in ancient Egypt

Mixed-Up Files Vocabulary Word List Continued

No. Word	Clue/Definition
44. MUTUAL	Shared
45. MUZZLED	Prevented a person from speaking, especially in public
46. ORNATELY	Elaborately or elegantly decorated
47. ORTHOPEDIC	Relating to disorders of the bones, joints, ligaments, or muscles
48. PAUPERS	Extremely poor individuals
49. PEER	To look carefully, especially with narrowed eyes
50. PERSUADE	To convince or make someone believe something
51. PHARAOH	A king of ancient Egypt
52. PREOCCUPIED	Totally absorbed in doing or thinking about something else
53. PROMPTED	Urged
54. PUBLICITY	Public interest or knowledge
55. PUNCTUATED	To end with emphasis
56. QUARRIED	Obtained or gotten after much effort
57. REGARD	To think of a person or thing in a particular way
58. SARCOPHAGUS	An ancient stone or marble coffin
59. SCOLDING	Complaining, especially when using harsh language
60. SCOWLED	Made a facial expression characterized by drawing the eyebrows together in anger or displeasure
61. SCREECHED	Made a loud, high-pitched sound
62. SEEPED	Passed through an opening very slowly
63. SHEPHERDED	Guided a group of people or animals
64. SHRUNKEN	Characterized by a decrease in size
65. SHUFFLING	To walk without picking up one's feet
66. SMUG	Conceited
67. STAMMERED	Spoke with many hesitations due to fear or strong emotion
68. STEALTHILY	Secretively or cunningly
69. STOWAWAY	Someone who hides on a traveling vessel in hopes of gaining passage without paying
70. SUMMONED	Sent for someone to come
71. THEATRICS	Display of false and exaggerated emotion
72. TRANSPORTED	Moved someone or something from one place to another, especially in a vehicle
73. TYRANNIES	Cruelties suffered at the hand of people in authority
74. VENDOR	Someone who sells something
75. VETO	To exercise the right to reject something

Mixed-Up Files Vocabulary Fill-in-the-Blanks 1

_____ 1. A king of ancient Egypt

_____ 2. Gave something to somebody as his or her share of what is available

_____ 3. An afternoon performance of a play, usually with cheaper seats than the evening performance

_____ 4. An explanation at the bottom of a page giving further information about something in the text above

_____ 5. Unfair treatment

_____ 6. Someone who hides on a traveling vessel in hopes of gaining passage without paying

_____ 7. Relating to disorders of the bones, joints, ligaments, or muscles

_____ 8. Bodies of people that have been embalmed and wrapped in cloth, as was the custom in ancient Egypt

_____ 9. To say something that contradicts what someone else has said

_____ 10. Complaining, especially when using harsh language

_____ 11. Revealing or telling about

_____ 12. Something completed something else, or made it close to perfect

_____ 13. Elaborately or elegantly decorated

_____ 14. A mixture of several unrelated things

_____ 15. Someone who pretends to be someone he is not

_____ 16. Giving credit to a person for a particular piece of art or work of literature

_____ 17. Extremely poor individuals

_____ 18. Went upward

_____ 19. The act of complimenting someone for the purpose of getting something

_____ 20. Connected to or having to do with

Mixed-Up Files Vocabulary Fill-in-the-Blanks 1 Answer Key

PHARAOH	1. A king of ancient Egypt
ALLOTTED	2. Gave something to somebody as his or her share of what is available
MATINEE	3. An afternoon performance of a play, usually with cheaper seats than the evening performance
FOOTNOTES	4. An explanation at the bottom of a page giving further information about something in the text above
INJUSTICE	5. Unfair treatment
STOWAWAY	6. Someone who hides on a traveling vessel in hopes of gaining passage without paying
ORTHOPEDIC	7. Relating to disorders of the bones, joints, ligaments, or muscles
MUMMIES	8. Bodies of people that have been embalmed and wrapped in cloth, as was the custom in ancient Egypt
COUNTERED	9. To say something that contradicts what someone else has said
SCOLDING	10. Complaining, especially when using harsh language
DISCLOSING	11. Revealing or telling about
COMPLEMENTED	12. Something completed something else, or made it close to perfect
ORNATELY	13. Elaborately or elegantly decorated
HODGEPODGE	14. A mixture of several unrelated things
IMPOSTER	15. Someone who pretends to be someone he is not
ATTRIBUTING	16. Giving credit to a person for a particular piece of art or work of literature
PAUPERS	17. Extremely poor individuals
ASCENDED	18. Went upward
FLATTERY	19. The act of complimenting someone for the purpose of getting something
ASSOCIATED	20. Connected to or having to do with

Mixed-Up Files Vocabulary Fill-in-the-Blanks 2

_____ 1. To say something that contradicts what someone else has said
_____ 2. Driver
_____ 3. Made a loud, high-pitched sound
_____ 4. Giving credit to a person for a particular piece of art or work of literature
_____ 5. To look carefully, especially with narrowed eyes
_____ 6. Collected over time until they form a large fund
_____ 7. Urged
_____ 8. Display of false and exaggerated emotion
_____ 9. Public interest or knowledge
_____ 10. Looking around in a leisurely manner
_____ 11. Pointed someone in a particular direction
_____ 12. Conceited
_____ 13. A mixture of several unrelated things
_____ 14. Secretively or cunningly
_____ 15. Prevented a person from speaking, especially in public
_____ 16. Areas of the skin that has been hurt by scraping
_____ 17. An ancient stone or marble coffin
_____ 18. Revealing or telling about
_____ 19. Freedom to think or act
_____ 20. Revealed

Mixed-Up Files Vocabulary Fill-in-the-Blanks 2 Answer Key

COUNTERED	1. To say something that contradicts what someone else has said
CHAUFFEUR	2. Driver
SCREECHED	3. Made a loud, high-pitched sound
ATTRIBUTING	4. Giving credit to a person for a particular piece of art or work of literature
PEER	5. To look carefully, especially with narrowed eyes
AMASSED	6. Collected over time until they form a large fund
PROMPTED	7. Urged
THEATRICS	8. Display of false and exaggerated emotion
PUBLICITY	9. Public interest or knowledge
BROWSING	10. Looking around in a leisurely manner
DIRECTED	11. Pointed someone in a particular direction
SMUG	12. Conceited
HODGEPODGE	13. A mixture of several unrelated things
STEALTHILY	14. Secretively or cunningly
MUZZLED	15. Prevented a person from speaking, especially in public
ABRASIONS	16. Areas of the skin that has been hurt by scraping
SARCOPHAGUS	17. An ancient stone or marble coffin
DISCLOSING	18. Revealing or telling about
LIBERTY	19. Freedom to think or act
EXPOSED	20. Revealed

Mixed-Up Files Vocabulary Fill-in-the-Blanks 3

1. To officially release students from school
2. Characterized by a decrease in size
3. To exercise the right to reject something
4. Conceited
5. Someone who hides on a traveling vessel in hopes of gaining passage without paying
6. The act of complimenting someone for the purpose of getting something
7. To rain lightly
8. Spoke with many hesitations due to fear or strong emotion
9. A light-hearted adventure or a dangerous illegal activity
10. To end with emphasis
11. Complaining, especially when using harsh language
12. Sent for someone to come
13. Freedom to think or act
14. Become used to a certain thing or way of doing things
15. Someone who sells something
16. Made a loud, high-pitched sound
17. Precise and correct
18. Collected over time until they form a large fund
19. Made a facial expression characterized by drawing the eyebrows together in anger or displeasure
20. Urged

Mixed-Up Files Vocabulary Fill-in-the-Blanks 3 Answer Key

DISMISS	1. To officially release students from school
SHRUNKEN	2. Characterized by a decrease in size
VETO	3. To exercise the right to reject something
SMUG	4. Conceited
STOWAWAY	5. Someone who hides on a traveling vessel in hopes of gaining passage without paying
FLATTERY	6. The act of complimenting someone for the purpose of getting something
DRIZZLE	7. To rain lightly
STAMMERED	8. Spoke with many hesitations due to fear or strong emotion
CAPER	9. A light-hearted adventure or a dangerous illegal activity
PUNCTUATED	10. To end with emphasis
SCOLDING	11. Complaining, especially when using harsh language
SUMMONED	12. Sent for someone to come
LIBERTY	13. Freedom to think or act
ACCUSTOMED	14. Become used to a certain thing or way of doing things
VENDOR	15. Someone who sells something
SCREECHED	16. Made a loud, high-pitched sound
ACCURATE	17. Precise and correct
AMASSED	18. Collected over time until they form a large fund
SCOWLED	19. Made a facial expression characterized by drawing the eyebrows together in anger or displeasure
PROMPTED	20. Urged

Mixed-Up Files Vocabulary Fill-in-the-Blanks 4

1. Looking around in a leisurely manner
2. An ancient stone or marble coffin
3. Pointed someone in a particular direction
4. Someone who hides on a traveling vessel in hopes of gaining passage without paying
5. A light-hearted adventure or a dangerous illegal activity
6. A king of ancient Egypt
7. Totally absorbed in doing or thinking about something else
8. Shared
9. Areas of the skin that has been hurt by scraping
10. Unfair treatment
11. Freedom to think or act
12. To say something that contradicts what someone else has said
13. To make someone very interested
14. To end with emphasis
15. Revealed
16. Spoke with many hesitations due to fear or strong emotion
17. Precise and correct
18. An explanation at the bottom of a page giving further information about something in the text above
19. A feeling of modesty
20. Moved someone or something from one place to another, especially in a vehicle

Mixed-Up Files Vocabulary Fill-in-the-Blanks 4 Answer Key

BROWSING	1. Looking around in a leisurely manner
SARCOPHAGUS	2. An ancient stone or marble coffin
DIRECTED	3. Pointed someone in a particular direction
STOWAWAY	4. Someone who hides on a traveling vessel in hopes of gaining passage without paying
CAPER	5. A light-hearted adventure or a dangerous illegal activity
PHARAOH	6. A king of ancient Egypt
PREOCCUPIED	7. Totally absorbed in doing or thinking about something else
MUTUAL	8. Shared
ABRASIONS	9. Areas of the skin that has been hurt by scraping
INJUSTICE	10. Unfair treatment
LIBERTY	11. Freedom to think or act
COUNTERED	12. To say something that contradicts what someone else has said
INTRIGUED	13. To make someone very interested
PUNCTUATED	14. To end with emphasis
EXPOSED	15. Revealed
STAMMERED	16. Spoke with many hesitations due to fear or strong emotion
ACCURATE	17. Precise and correct
FOOTNOTES	18. An explanation at the bottom of a page giving further information about something in the text above
HUMILITY	19. A feeling of modesty
TRANSPORTED	20. Moved someone or something from one place to another, especially in a vehicle

Mixed-Up Files Vocabulary Matching 1

___ 1. PUNCTUATED A. An afternoon performance of a play, usually with cheaper seats than the evening performance
___ 2. FOOTNOTES B. To end with emphasis
___ 3. ALLOTTED C. Someone who pretends to be someone he is not
___ 4. ORNATELY D. The act of complimenting someone for the purpose of getting something
___ 5. MUMMIES E. Become used to a certain thing or way of doing things
___ 6. EMERGE F. Gave something to somebody as his or her share of what is available
___ 7. PERSUADE G. Spoke with many hesitations due to fear or strong emotion
___ 8. PAUPERS H. Bodies of people that have been embalmed and wrapped in cloth, as was the custom in ancient Egypt
___ 9. VENDOR I. Elaborately or elegantly decorated
___ 10. MATINEE J. Someone who sells something
___ 11. SARCOPHAGUS K. To appear
___ 12. QUARRIED L. To exercise the right to reject something
___ 13. IMPOSTER M. An ancient stone or marble coffin
___ 14. ACCUSTOMED N. Pointed someone in a particular direction
___ 15. PREOCCUPIED O. Driver
___ 16. MEDIOCRE P. Adequate, but not very good
___ 17. STAMMERED Q. A king of ancient Egypt
___ 18. PHARAOH R. Obtained or gotten after much effort
___ 19. SHUFFLING S. An explanation at the bottom of a page giving further information about something in the text above
___ 20. STEALTHILY T. Cruelties suffered at the hand of people in authority
___ 21. CHAUFFEUR U. Secretively or cunningly
___ 22. FLATTERY V. To convince or make someone believe something
___ 23. DIRECTED W. To walk without picking up one's feet
___ 24. TYRANNIES X. Extremely poor individuals
___ 25. VETO Y. Totally absorbed in doing or thinking about something else

Mixed-Up Files Vocabulary Matching 1 Answer Key

B - 1.	PUNCTUATED	A. An afternoon performance of a play, usually with cheaper seats than the evening performance
S - 2.	FOOTNOTES	B. To end with emphasis
F - 3.	ALLOTTED	C. Someone who pretends to be someone he is not
I - 4.	ORNATELY	D. The act of complimenting someone for the purpose of getting something
H - 5.	MUMMIES	E. Become used to a certain thing or way of doing things
K - 6.	EMERGE	F. Gave something to somebody as his or her share of what is available
V - 7.	PERSUADE	G. Spoke with many hesitations due to fear or strong emotion
X - 8.	PAUPERS	H. Bodies of people that have been embalmed and wrapped in cloth, as was the custom in ancient Egypt
J - 9.	VENDOR	I. Elaborately or elegantly decorated
A - 10.	MATINEE	J. Someone who sells something
M - 11.	SARCOPHAGUS	K. To appear
R - 12.	QUARRIED	L. To exercise the right to reject something
C - 13.	IMPOSTER	M. An ancient stone or marble coffin
E - 14.	ACCUSTOMED	N. Pointed someone in a particular direction
Y - 15.	PREOCCUPIED	O. Driver
P - 16.	MEDIOCRE	P. Adequate, but not very good
G - 17.	STAMMERED	Q. A king of ancient Egypt
Q - 18.	PHARAOH	R. Obtained or gotten after much effort
W - 19.	SHUFFLING	S. An explanation at the bottom of a page giving further information about something in the text above
U - 20.	STEALTHILY	T. Cruelties suffered at the hand of people in authority
O - 21.	CHAUFFEUR	U. Secretively or cunningly
D - 22.	FLATTERY	V. To convince or make someone believe something
N - 23.	DIRECTED	W. To walk without picking up one's feet
T - 24.	TYRANNIES	X. Extremely poor individuals
L - 25.	VETO	Y. Totally absorbed in doing or thinking about something else

Mixed-Up Files Vocabulary Matching 2

___ 1. PAUPERS   A. Driver
___ 2. LIBERTY   B. Adequate, but not very good
___ 3. DIRECTED   C. Become used to a certain thing or way of doing things
___ 4. PERSUADE   D. Pointed someone in a particular direction
___ 5. SEEPED   E. Spoke with many hesitations due to fear or strong emotion
___ 6. CAPER   F. To think of a person or thing in a particular way
___ 7. DISMISS   G. Gave something to somebody as his or her share of what is available
___ 8. DISCLOSING   H. Bodies of people that have been embalmed and wrapped in cloth, as was the custom in ancient Egypt
___ 9. MUMMIES   I. Someone who hides on a traveling vessel in hopes of gaining passage without paying
___10. STOWAWAY   J. A young person who has broken the law
___11. DRIZZLE   K. To convince or make someone believe something
___12. THEATRICS   L. Passed through an opening very slowly
___13. SCREECHED   M. To rain lightly
___14. REGARD   N. A king of ancient Egypt
___15. PHARAOH   O. Extremely poor individuals
___16. VENDOR   P. Revealing or telling about
___17. TYRANNIES   Q. Display of false and exaggerated emotion
___18. ACCUSTOMED   R. Freedom to think or act
___19. DELINQUENT   S. To officially release students from school
___20. SCOWLED   T. A light-hearted adventure or a dangerous illegal activity
___21. STAMMERED   U. Someone who sells something
___22. MEDIOCRE   V. Made a loud, high-pitched sound
___23. MONOTONY   W. Cruelties suffered at the hand of people in authority
___24. ALLOTTED   X. Made a facial expression characterized by drawing the eyebrows together in anger or displeasure
___25. CHAUFFEUR   Y. boredom that comes from doing the same thing over and over

Mixed-Up Files Vocabulary Matching 2 Answer Key

O - 1. PAUPERS	A.	Driver
R - 2. LIBERTY	B.	Adequate, but not very good
D - 3. DIRECTED	C.	Become used to a certain thing or way of doing things
K - 4. PERSUADE	D.	Pointed someone in a particular direction
L - 5. SEEPED	E.	Spoke with many hesitations due to fear or strong emotion
T - 6. CAPER	F.	To think of a person or thing in a particular way
S - 7. DISMISS	G.	Gave something to somebody as his or her share of what is available
P - 8. DISCLOSING	H.	Bodies of people that have been embalmed and wrapped in cloth, as was the custom in ancient Egypt
H - 9. MUMMIES	I.	Someone who hides on a traveling vessel in hopes of gaining passage without paying
I - 10. STOWAWAY	J.	A young person who has broken the law
M - 11. DRIZZLE	K.	To convince or make someone believe something
Q - 12. THEATRICS	L.	Passed through an opening very slowly
V - 13. SCREECHED	M.	To rain lightly
F - 14. REGARD	N.	A king of ancient Egypt
N - 15. PHARAOH	O.	Extremely poor individuals
U - 16. VENDOR	P.	Revealing or telling about
W - 17. TYRANNIES	Q.	Display of false and exaggerated emotion
C - 18. ACCUSTOMED	R.	Freedom to think or act
J - 19. DELINQUENT	S.	To officially release students from school
X - 20. SCOWLED	T.	A light-hearted adventure or a dangerous illegal activity
E - 21. STAMMERED	U.	Someone who sells something
B - 22. MEDIOCRE	V.	Made a loud, high-pitched sound
Y - 23. MONOTONY	W.	Cruelties suffered at the hand of people in authority
G - 24. ALLOTTED	X.	Made a facial expression characterized by drawing the eyebrows together in anger or displeasure
A - 25. CHAUFFEUR	Y.	boredom that comes from doing the same thing over and over

Mixed-Up Files Vocabulary Matching 3

___ 1. SMUG
___ 2. ASSOCIATED
___ 3. COUNTERED
___ 4. SARCOPHAGUS
___ 5. MEDIOCRE
___ 6. VENDOR
___ 7. ALLOTTED
___ 8. HUMILITY
___ 9. ACCUSTOMED
___ 10. CLAMPED
___ 11. DISMALLY
___ 12. QUARRIED
___ 13. MUMMIES
___ 14. ORNATELY
___ 15. PERSUADE
___ 16. HODGEPODGE
___ 17. SHUFFLING
___ 18. STOWAWAY
___ 19. SCOWLED
___ 20. BAROQUE
___ 21. VETO
___ 22. DIRECTED
___ 23. MAIMED
___ 24. EXPOSED
___ 25. KEEN

A. Adequate, but not very good
B. To walk without picking up one's feet
C. To say something that contradicts what someone else has said
D. Elaborately or elegantly decorated
E. Become used to a certain thing or way of doing things
F. Pointed someone in a particular direction
G. A mixture of several unrelated things
H. Bodies of people that have been embalmed and wrapped in cloth, as was the custom in ancient Egypt
I. Gave something to somebody as his or her share of what is available
J. Revealed
K. An ancient stone or marble coffin
L. A feeling of modesty
M. In a depressing manner
N. Conceited
O. Held tightly over
P. Made a facial expression characterized by drawing the eyebrows together in anger or displeasure
Q. To exercise the right to reject something
R. Obtained or gotten after much effort
S. Connected to or having to do with
T. An ornamental style of European art (mid-16th to early 18th centuries)
U. Slang term for very cool
V. To convince or make someone believe something
W. Someone who sells something
X. Someone who hides on a traveling vessel in hopes of gaining passage without paying
Y. Affected with a severe and permanent injury

Mixed-Up Files Vocabulary Matching 3 Answer Key

N - 1.	SMUG	A.	Adequate, but not very good
S - 2.	ASSOCIATED	B.	To walk without picking up one's feet
C - 3.	COUNTERED	C.	To say something that contradicts what someone else has said
K - 4.	SARCOPHAGUS	D.	Elaborately or elegantly decorated
A - 5.	MEDIOCRE	E.	Become used to a certain thing or way of doing things
W - 6.	VENDOR	F.	Pointed someone in a particular direction
I - 7.	ALLOTTED	G.	A mixture of several unrelated things
L - 8.	HUMILITY	H.	Bodies of people that have been embalmed and wrapped in cloth, as was the custom in ancient Egypt
E - 9.	ACCUSTOMED	I.	Gave something to somebody as his or her share of what is available
O -10.	CLAMPED	J.	Revealed
M -11.	DISMALLY	K.	An ancient stone or marble coffin
R -12.	QUARRIED	L.	A feeling of modesty
H -13.	MUMMIES	M.	In a depressing manner
D -14.	ORNATELY	N.	Conceited
V -15.	PERSUADE	O.	Held tightly over
G -16.	HODGEPODGE	P.	Made a facial expression characterized by drawing the eyebrows together in anger or displeasure
B -17.	SHUFFLING	Q.	To exercise the right to reject something
X -18.	STOWAWAY	R.	Obtained or gotten after much effort
P -19.	SCOWLED	S.	Connected to or having to do with
T -20.	BAROQUE	T.	An ornamental style of European art (mid-16th to early 18th centuries)
Q -21.	VETO	U.	Slang term for very cool
F -22.	DIRECTED	V.	To convince or make someone believe something
Y -23.	MAIMED	W.	Someone who sells something
J -24.	EXPOSED	X.	Someone who hides on a traveling vessel in hopes of gaining passage without paying
U -25.	KEEN	Y.	Affected with a severe and permanent injury

Mixed-Up Files Vocabulary Matching 4

___ 1. AMASSED   A. Someone who sells something

___ 2. BAROQUE   B. Moved someone or something from one place to another, especially in a vehicle

___ 3. ORNATELY   C. Looking around in a leisurely manner

___ 4. IMPOSTER   D. Held tightly over

___ 5. COMMOTION   E. Something completed something else, or made it close to perfect

___ 6. PHARAOH   F. To appear

___ 7. BROWSING   G. A king of ancient Egypt

___ 8. PEER   H. A young person who has broken the law

___ 9. ADVISED   I. Guided a group of people or animals

___10. REGARD   J. Shared

___11. DELINQUENT   K. Public interest or knowledge

___12. SHEPHERDED   L. Elaborately or elegantly decorated

___13. CAPER   M. To officially release students from school

___14. EMERGE   N. Become used to a certain thing or way of doing things

___15. MAIMED   O. Recommended

___16. ACCUSTOMED   P. Revealed

___17. COMPLEMENTED   Q. Affected with a severe and permanent injury

___18. PUBLICITY   R. Adequate, but not very good

___19. TRANSPORTED   S. To look carefully, especially with narrowed eyes

___20. VENDOR   T. A light-hearted adventure or a dangerous illegal activity

___21. DISMISS   U. Collected over time until they form a large fund

___22. CLAMPED   V. Noisy activity or confusion

___23. MEDIOCRE   W. Someone who pretends to be someone he is not

___24. EXPOSED   X. An ornamental style of European art (mid-16th to early 18th centuries)

___25. MUTUAL   Y. To think of a person or thing in a particular way

Mixed-Up Files Vocabulary Matching 4 Answer Key

U - 1.	AMASSED	A. Someone who sells something
X - 2.	BAROQUE	B. Moved someone or something from one place to another, especially in a vehicle
L - 3.	ORNATELY	C. Looking around in a leisurely manner
W - 4.	IMPOSTER	D. Held tightly over
V - 5.	COMMOTION	E. Something completed something else, or made it close to perfect
G - 6.	PHARAOH	F. To appear
C - 7.	BROWSING	G. A king of ancient Egypt
S - 8.	PEER	H. A young person who has broken the law
O - 9.	ADVISED	I. Guided a group of people or animals
Y - 10.	REGARD	J. Shared
H - 11.	DELINQUENT	K. Public interest or knowledge
I - 12.	SHEPHERDED	L. Elaborately or elegantly decorated
T - 13.	CAPER	M. To officially release students from school
F - 14.	EMERGE	N. Become used to a certain thing or way of doing things
Q - 15.	MAIMED	O. Recommended
N - 16.	ACCUSTOMED	P. Revealed
E - 17.	COMPLEMENTED	Q. Affected with a severe and permanent injury
K - 18.	PUBLICITY	R. Adequate, but not very good
B - 19.	TRANSPORTED	S. To look carefully, especially with narrowed eyes
A - 20.	VENDOR	T. A light-hearted adventure or a dangerous illegal activity
M - 21.	DISMISS	U. Collected over time until they form a large fund
D - 22.	CLAMPED	V. Noisy activity or confusion
R - 23.	MEDIOCRE	W. Someone who pretends to be someone he is not
P - 24.	EXPOSED	X. An ornamental style of European art (mid-16th to early 18th centuries)
J - 25.	MUTUAL	Y. To think of a person or thing in a particular way

Mixed-Up Files Vocabulary Magic Squares 1

Match the definition with the vocabulary word. Put your answers in the magic squares below. When your answers are correct, all columns and rows will add to the same number.

A. SUMMONED
B. SCOWLED
C. EXPOSED
D. ORNATELY
E. SCREECHED
F. AMASSED
G. IMPOSTER
H. MAIMED
I. INJUSTICE
J. MATINEE
K. ABRASIONS
L. BROWSING
M. SHEPHERDED
N. ATTRIBUTING
O. COUNTERED
P. CHAUFFEUR

1. Sent for someone to come
2. Giving credit to a person for a particular piece of art or work of literature
3. An afternoon performance of a play, usually with cheaper seats than the evening performance
4. Made a loud, high-pitched sound
5. Someone who pretends to be someone he is not
6. Looking around in a leisurely manner
7. Driver
8. Revealed
9. To say something that contradicts what someone else has said
10. Elaborately or elegantly decorated
11. Affected with a severe and permanent injury
12. Areas of the skin that has been hurt by scraping
13. Unfair treatment
14. Collected over time until they form a large fund
15. Made a facial expression characterized by drawing the eyebrows together in anger or displeasure
16. Guided a group of people or animals

A=	B=	C=	D=
E=	F=	G=	H=
I=	J=	K=	L=
M=	N=	O=	P=

Mixed-Up Files Vocabulary Magic Squares 1 Answer Key

Match the definition with the vocabulary word. Put your answers in the magic squares below. When your answers are correct, all columns and rows will add to the same number.

A. SUMMONED
B. SCOWLED
C. EXPOSED
D. ORNATELY
E. SCREECHED
F. AMASSED
G. IMPOSTER
H. MAIMED
I. INJUSTICE
J. MATINEE
K. ABRASIONS
L. BROWSING
M. SHEPHERDED
N. ATTRIBUTING
O. COUNTERED
P. CHAUFFEUR

1. Sent for someone to come
2. Giving credit to a person for a particular piece of art or work of literature
3. An afternoon performance of a play, usually with cheaper seats than the evening performance
4. Made a loud, high-pitched sound
5. Someone who pretends to be someone he is not
6. Looking around in a leisurely manner
7. Driver
8. Revealed
9. To say something that contradicts what someone else has said
10. Elaborately or elegantly decorated
11. Affected with a severe and permanent injury
12. Areas of the skin that has been hurt by scraping
13. Unfair treatment
14. Collected over time until they form a large fund
15. Made a facial expression characterized by drawing the eyebrows together in anger or displeasure
16. Guided a group of people or animals

A=1	B=15	C=8	D=10
E=4	F=14	G=5	H=11
I=13	J=3	K=12	L=6
M=16	N=2	O=9	P=7

Mixed-Up Files Vocabulary Magic Squares 2

Match the definition with the vocabulary word. Put your answers in the magic squares below. When your answers are correct, all columns and rows will add to the same number.

A. DESCENDING
B. PAUPERS
C. SEEPED
D. ADVISED
E. SHRUNKEN
F. PHARAOH
G. FLATTERY
H. DECEASED
I. ACCURATE
J. THEATRICS
K. MATINEE
L. KEEN
M. ABRASIONS
N. MUZZLED
O. ATTRIBUTING
P. CLAMPED

1. Giving credit to a person for a particular piece of art or work of literature
2. Recommended
3. Display of false and exaggerated emotion
4. Characterized by a decrease in size
5. Precise and correct
6. A king of ancient Egypt
7. Held tightly over
8. Passed through an opening very slowly
9. Dead
10. An afternoon performance of a play, usually with cheaper seats than the evening performance
11. Coming down
12. Prevented a person from speaking, especially in public
13. Extremely poor individuals
14. Areas of the skin that has been hurt by scraping
15. The act of complimenting someone for the purpose of getting something
16. Slang term for very cool

A=	B=	C=	D=
E=	F=	G=	H=
I=	J=	K=	L=
M=	N=	O=	P=

Mixed-Up Files Vocabulary Magic Squares 2 Answer Key

Match the definition with the vocabulary word. Put your answers in the magic squares below. When your answers are correct, all columns and rows will add to the same number.

A. DESCENDING
B. PAUPERS
C. SEEPED
D. ADVISED
E. SHRUNKEN
F. PHARAOH
G. FLATTERY
H. DECEASED
I. ACCURATE
J. THEATRICS
K. MATINEE
L. KEEN
M. ABRASIONS
N. MUZZLED
O. ATTRIBUTING
P. CLAMPED

1. Giving credit to a person for a particular piece of art or work of literature
2. Recommended
3. Display of false and exaggerated emotion
4. Characterized by a decrease in size
5. Precise and correct
6. A king of ancient Egypt
7. Held tightly over
8. Passed through an opening very slowly
9. Dead
10. An afternoon performance of a play, usually with cheaper seats than the evening performance
11. Coming down
12. Prevented a person from speaking, especially in public
13. Extremely poor individuals
14. Areas of the skin that has been hurt by scraping
15. The act of complimenting someone for the purpose of getting something
16. Slang term for very cool

A=11	B=13	C=8	D=2
E=4	F=6	G=15	H=9
I=5	J=3	K=10	L=16
M=14	N=12	O=1	P=7

Mixed-Up Files Vocabulary Magic Squares 3

Match the definition with the vocabulary word. Put your answers in the magic squares below. When your answers are correct, all columns and rows will add to the same number.

A. SHEPHERDED
B. SHUFFLING
C. INTRIGUED
D. PREOCCUPIED
E. MUTUAL
F. PAUPERS
G. INJUSTICE
H. ORNATELY
I. ADVISED
J. ACCURATE
K. SMUG
L. EXPOSED
M. VETO
N. MUMMIES
O. COMMOTION
P. SCOLDING

1. To exercise the right to reject something
2. Extremely poor individuals
3. Elaborately or elegantly decorated
4. Noisy activity or confusion
5. Revealed
6. To make someone very interested
7. Guided a group of people or animals
8. Precise and correct
9. Conceited
10. Totally absorbed in doing or thinking about something else
11. To walk without picking up one's feet
12. Recommended
13. Bodies of people that have been embalmed and wrapped in cloth, as was the custom in ancient Egypt
14. Shared
15. Unfair treatment
16. Complaining, especially when using harsh language

A=	B=	C=	D=
E=	F=	G=	H=
I=	J=	K=	L=
M=	N=	O=	P=

Mixed-Up Files Vocabulary Magic Squares 3 Answer Key

Match the definition with the vocabulary word. Put your answers in the magic squares below. When your answers are correct, all columns and rows will add to the same number.

A. SHEPHERDED
B. SHUFFLING
C. INTRIGUED
D. PREOCCUPIED
E. MUTUAL
F. PAUPERS
G. INJUSTICE
H. ORNATELY
I. ADVISED
J. ACCURATE
K. SMUG
L. EXPOSED
M. VETO
N. MUMMIES
O. COMMOTION
P. SCOLDING

1. To exercise the right to reject something
2. Extremely poor individuals
3. Elaborately or elegantly decorated
4. Noisy activity or confusion
5. Revealed
6. To make someone very interested
7. Guided a group of people or animals
8. Precise and correct
9. Conceited
10. Totally absorbed in doing or thinking about something else
11. To walk without picking up one's feet
12. Recommended
13. Bodies of people that have been embalmed and wrapped in cloth, as was the custom in ancient Egypt
14. Shared
15. Unfair treatment
16. Complaining, especially when using harsh language

A=7	B=11	C=6	D=10
E=14	F=2	G=15	H=3
I=12	J=8	K=9	L=5
M=1	N=13	O=4	P=16

Mixed-Up Files Vocabulary Magic Squares 4

Match the definition with the vocabulary word. Put your answers in the magic squares below. When your answers are correct, all columns and rows will add to the same number.

A. MASTABA
B. COMMOTION
C. MAIMED
D. CHAUFFEUR
E. INJUSTICE
F. COMPLEMENTED
G. QUARRIED
H. REGARD
I. PUBLICITY
J. FLATTERY
K. MONOTONY
L. SHEPHERDED
M. BAROQUE
N. SEEPED
O. TRANSPORTED
P. ACCUSTOMED

1. Something completed something else, or made it close to perfect
2. Public interest or knowledge
3. Moved someone or something from one place to another, especially in a vehicle
4. Driver
5. An ornamental style of European art (mid-16th to early 18th centuries)
6. Noisy activity or confusion
7. To think of a person or thing in a particular way
8. boredom that comes from doing the same thing over and over
9. Affected with a severe and permanent injury
10. Become used to a certain thing or way of doing things
11. The act of complimenting someone for the purpose of getting something
12. Unfair treatment
13. Guided a group of people or animals
14. Obtained or gotten after much effort
15. An ancient Egyptian tomb with a flat base, sloping sides, and a flat roof
16. Passed through an opening very slowly

A=	B=	C=	D=
E=	F=	G=	H=
I=	J=	K=	L=
M=	N=	O=	P=

Mixed-Up Files Vocabulary Magic Squares 4 Answer Key

Match the definition with the vocabulary word. Put your answers in the magic squares below. When your answers are correct, all columns and rows will add to the same number.

A. MASTABA
B. COMMOTION
C. MAIMED
D. CHAUFFEUR
E. INJUSTICE
F. COMPLEMENTED
G. QUARRIED
H. REGARD
I. PUBLICITY
J. FLATTERY
K. MONOTONY
L. SHEPHERDED
M. BAROQUE
N. SEEPED
O. TRANSPORTED
P. ACCUSTOMED

1. Something completed something else, or made it close to perfect
2. Public interest or knowledge
3. Moved someone or something from one place to another, especially in a vehicle
4. Driver
5. An ornamental style of European art (mid-16th to early 18th centuries)
6. Noisy activity or confusion
7. To think of a person or thing in a particular way
8. boredom that comes from doing the same thing over and over
9. Affected with a severe and permanent injury
10. Become used to a certain thing or way of doing things
11. The act of complimenting someone for the purpose of getting something
12. Unfair treatment
13. Guided a group of people or animals
14. Obtained or gotten after much effort
15. An ancient Egyptian tomb with a flat base, sloping sides, and a flat roof
16. Passed through an opening very slowly

A=15	B=6	C=9	D=4
E=12	F=1	G=14	H=7
I=2	J=11	K=8	L=13
M=5	N=16	O=3	P=10

Mixed-Up Files Vocabulary Word Search 1

```
D K P N L I B E R T Y C O M M O T I O N
O R Y X H C A D I S M A L L Y A B S D D
S R I C Z O R H I N J U S T I C E C F S
T N N Z X M O M E D I O C R E C B O Q X
A X A A Z P Q Q J Y H X O A G U W W U W
M C T T T L U B G K M O L K M R J L A V
M A T I N E E R E G A R D E C A P E R R
E E R C M M L C B Z D V I G M T S D R Z
R X I B Q E D Y S J E E N S E E Y S I F
E P B J S N G N Q V C N G U Q P R H E S
D O U I N T R I G U E D M M K P O G D D
J S T K C E E H J Q A O U M M E P D E T
P E I C S D D A H F S R Z O U R E G G W
V D N D L M S I L X E K Z N M S E N G E
P E G Y L A U E S T D D L E M U R K M B
T S T C G I M G E M H H E D I A T J C K
W B X O V M H P M P I I D N E D L U R Y
S H E P H E R D E D E S L R S E M H A M
A S C E N D E D K D T D S Y J W Y J N L
```

A light-hearted adventure or a dangerous illegal activity (5)
A mixture of several unrelated things (10)
Adequate, but not very good (8)
Affected with a severe and permanent injury (6)
An afternoon performance of a play, usually with cheaper seats than the evening performance (7)
An ornamental style of European art (mid-16th to early 18th centuries) (7)
Bodies of people that have been embalmed and wrapped in cloth, as was the custom in ancient Egypt (7
Collected over time until they form a large fund (7)
Complaining, especially when using harsh language (8)
Conceited (4)
Dead (8)
Elaborately or elegantly decorated (8)
Freedom to think or act (7)
Giving credit to a person for a particular piece of art or work of literature (11)
Guided a group of people or animals (10)
Held tightly over (7)
In a depressing manner (8)
Made a facial expression characterized by drawing the eyebrows together in anger or displeasure (7)
Noisy activity or confusion (9)
Obtained or gotten after much effort (8)

Passed through an opening very slowly (6)
Precise and correct (8)
Prevented a person from speaking, especially in public (7)
Revealed (7)
Secretively or cunningly (10)
Sent for someone to come (8)
Shared (6)
Slang term for very cool (4)
Someone who sells something (6)
Something completed something else, or made it close to perfect (12)
Spoke with many hesitations due to fear or strong emotion (9)
To appear (6)
To convince or make someone believe something (8)
To exercise the right to reject something (4)
To look carefully, especially with narrowed eyes (4)
To make someone very interested (9)
To officially release students from school (7)
To rain lightly (7)
To think of a person or thing in a particular way (6)
Unfair treatment (9)
Went upward (8)

Mixed-Up Files Vocabulary Word Search 1 Answer Key

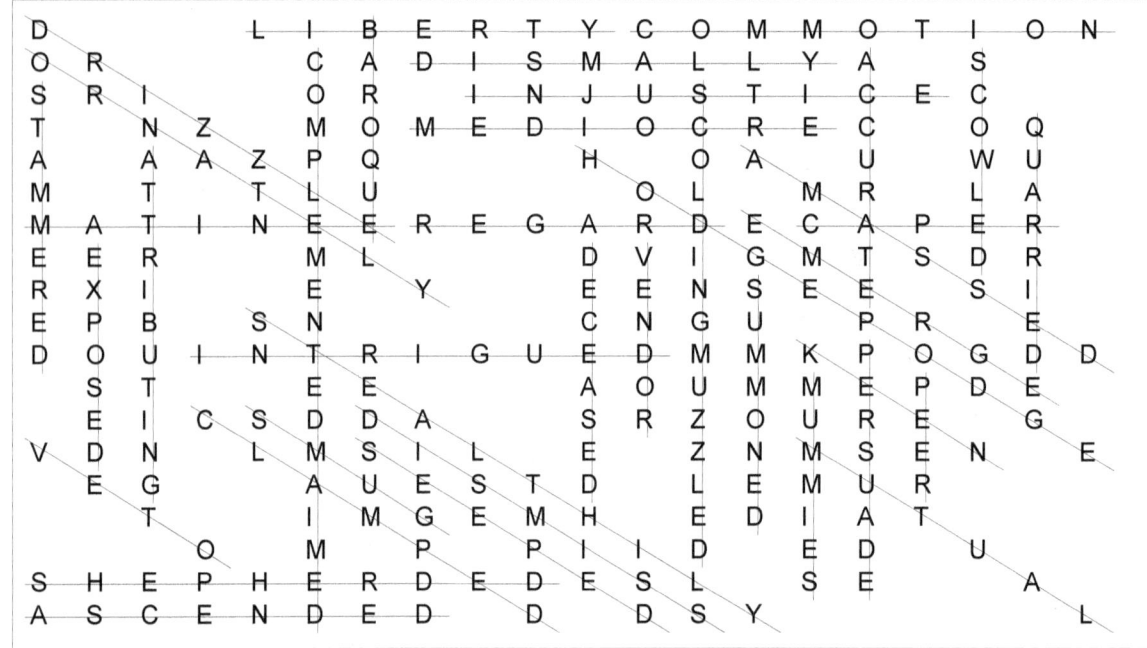

A light-hearted adventure or a dangerous illegal activity (5)
A mixture of several unrelated things (10)
Adequate, but not very good (8)
Affected with a severe and permanent injury (6)
An afternoon performance of a play, usually with cheaper seats than the evening performance (7)
An ornamental style of European art (mid-16th to early 18th centuries) (7)
Bodies of people that have been embalmed and wrapped in cloth, as was the custom in ancient Egypt (7)
Collected over time until they form a large fund (7)
Complaining, especially when using harsh language (8)
Conceited (4)
Dead (8)
Elaborately or elegantly decorated (8)
Freedom to think or act (7)
Giving credit to a person for a particular piece of art or work of literature (11)
Guided a group of people or animals (10)
Held tightly over (7)
In a depressing manner (8)
Made a facial expression characterized by drawing the eyebrows together in anger or displeasure (7)
Noisy activity or confusion (9)
Obtained or gotten after much effort (8)

Passed through an opening very slowly (6)
Precise and correct (8)
Prevented a person from speaking, especially in public (7)
Revealed (7)
Secretively or cunningly (10)
Sent for someone to come (8)
Shared (6)
Slang term for very cool (4)
Someone who sells something (6)
Something completed something else, or made it close to perfect (12)
Spoke with many hesitations due to fear or strong emotion (9)
To appear (6)
To convince or make someone believe something (8)
To exercise the right to reject something (4)
To look carefully, especially with narrowed eyes (4)
To make someone very interested (9)
To officially release students from school (7)
To rain lightly (7)
To think of a person or thing in a particular way (6)
Unfair treatment (9)
Went upward (8)

Mixed-Up Files Vocabulary Word Search 2

```
Q U A R R I E D A L E X P O S E D H P F
S Q M W K Y P E D I M S C M C E R K A K
L H J S R G R C V B E A X G O M E M U Y
W Q R W Y V O E I E R X S U B Q P P Q
M U T U A L M A S R G C J A N D Z A E J
C A V K N K P S E T E O C C T E V S R D
W L S A K K T E D Y K P O C E L B S S F
H S A C C S E D S R O H R U R I R O U L
N D T M E C D N R A R A N S E N O C M D
H C R O P N U M L L T G A T D Q W I M G
F U H I W E D R M L H U T O V U S A O M
M C M A Z A D E A O O S E M B E I T N Q
U E R I U Z W H D T P R L E A N N E E S
M T D E L F L A T T E R Y D M T G D D N
M S M I G I F E Y E D P P V P A I Q O F
I M P D O A T E M D I V R E E V I N K R
E U S G M C R Y U J C R Z W E T J M E V
S G C A P E R D I R E C T E D R O T E E
C O M P L E M E N T E D I S M I S S N D
```

A feeling of modesty (8)
A light-hearted adventure or a dangerous illegal activity (5)
A young person who has broken the law (10)
Adequate, but not very good (8)
Affected with a severe and permanent injury (6)
An afternoon performance of a play, usually with cheaper seats than the evening performance (7)
An ancient stone or marble coffin (11)
Become used to a certain thing or way of doing things (10)
Bodies of people that have been embalmed and wrapped in cloth, as was the custom in ancient Egypt (7)
Characterized by a decrease in size (8)
Conceited (4)
Connected to or having to do with (10)
Dead (8)
Driver (9)
Elaborately or elegantly decorated (8)
Extremely poor individuals (7)
Freedom to think or act (7)
Gave something to somebody as his or her share of what is available (8)
Held tightly over (7)
Looking around in a leisurely manner (8)
Obtained or gotten after much effort (8)
Passed through an opening very slowly (6)
Pointed someone in a particular direction (8)

Precise and correct (8)
Recommended (7)
Relating to disorders of the bones, joints, ligaments, or muscles (10)
Revealed (7)
Sent for someone to come (8)
Shared (6)
Slang term for very cool (4)
Someone who hides on a traveling vessel in hopes of gaining passage without paying (8)
Someone who sells something (6)
Something completed something else, or made it close to perfect (12)
The act of complimenting someone for the purpose of getting something (8)
To appear (6)
To exercise the right to reject something (4)
To look carefully, especially with narrowed eyes (4)
To officially release students from school (7)
To rain lightly (7)
To say something that contradicts what someone else has said (9)
To think of a person or thing in a particular way (6)
Urged (8)
Went upward (8)

Mixed-Up Files Vocabulary Word Search 2 Answer Key

A feeling of modesty (8)
A light-hearted adventure or a dangerous illegal activity (5)
A young person who has broken the law (10)
Adequate, but not very good (8)
Affected with a severe and permanent injury (6)
An afternoon performance of a play, usually with cheaper seats than the evening performance (7)
An ancient stone or marble coffin (11)
Become used to a certain thing or way of doing things (10)
Bodies of people that have been embalmed and wrapped in cloth, as was the custom in ancient Egypt (7
Characterized by a decrease in size (8)
Conceited (4)
Connected to or having to do with (10)
Dead (8)
Driver (9)
Elaborately or elegantly decorated (8)
Extremely poor individuals (7)
Freedom to think or act (7)
Gave something to somebody as his or her share of what is available (8)
Held tightly over (7)
Looking around in a leisurely manner (8)
Obtained or gotten after much effort (8)
Passed through an opening very slowly (6)
Pointed someone in a particular direction (8)

Precise and correct (8)
Recommended (7)
Relating to disorders of the bones, joints, ligaments, or muscles (10)
Revealed (7)
Sent for someone to come (8)
Shared (6)
Slang term for very cool (4)
Someone who hides on a traveling vessel in hopes of gaining passage without paying (8)
Someone who sells something (6)
Something completed something else, or made it close to perfect (12)
The act of complimenting someone for the purpose of getting something (8)
To appear (6)
To exercise the right to reject something (4)
To look carefully, especially with narrowed eyes (4)
To officially release students from school (7)
To rain lightly (7)
To say something that contradicts what someone else has said (9)
To think of a person or thing in a particular way (6)
Urged (8)
Went upward (8)

Mixed-Up Files Vocabulary Word Search 3

```
A S C E N D E D A N H S A T P V Z P V C
T Q U A R R I E D D G Q X L V E X R J D
R T F C P K L S E W V H Z N L T T O P F
S C O W L E D M C M A I M E D O M M A F
M H N Y K A C W E L N P S V K R T P U L
U A U Q Q Q M B A R O Q U E S T P T P R
G M S F V N X P S C V S X G D H R E E P
H A H M F L I B E R T Y I T H O E D R D
U S E C U L D G D D S W N N D P O D S L
M S P H V T I L Z S Z H T X G E C Z D R
I E H A X M U N R E G A R D V D C T I M
L D E U M H G A G E V S I U E I U Y S R
I X R F K U C C L P J T G S N C P R M J
T D D F R P M O T E E E U P D K I A I L
Y I E E L M T M Y D X A E E O D E N S X
F S D U N A K M I J P L D R R R D N S W
R M R R L S T O K E O T R S H I K I F V
C A P E R T P T E D S H M U Z Z L E D N
Y L C J Y A E I E Z E I K A N Z D S K D
P L T N K B E O N R D L Z D W L F F J S
T Y M P C A R N R S Y Y J E M E R G E V
```

ADVISED	DECEASED	INTRIGUED	PAUPERS	SHEPHERDED
ALLOTTED	DISCLOSING	KEEN	PEER	SHRUNKEN
AMASSED	DISMALLY	LIBERTY	PERSUADE	SHUFFLING
ASCENDED	DISMISS	MAIMED	PREOCCUPIED	SMUG
BAROQUE	DRIZZLE	MASTABA	PROMPTED	STEALTHILY
CAPER	EMERGE	MUMMIES	QUARRIED	TYRANNIES
CHAUFFEUR	EXPOSED	MUTUAL	REGARD	VENDOR
CLAMPED	FLATTERY	MUZZLED	SCOWLED	VETO
COMMOTION	HUMILITY	ORTHOPEDIC	SEEPED	

Mixed-Up Files Vocabulary Word Search 3 Answer Key

ADVISED	DECEASED	INTRIGUED	PAUPERS	SHEPHERDED
ALLOTTED	DISCLOSING	KEEN	PEER	SHRUNKEN
AMASSED	DISMALLY	LIBERTY	PERSUADE	SHUFFLING
ASCENDED	DISMISS	MAIMED	PREOCCUPIED	SMUG
BAROQUE	DRIZZLE	MASTABA	PROMPTED	STEALTHILY
CAPER	EMERGE	MUMMIES	QUARRIED	TYRANNIES
CHAUFFEUR	EXPOSED	MUTUAL	REGARD	VENDOR
CLAMPED	FLATTERY	MUZZLED	SCOWLED	VETO
COMMOTION	HUMILITY	ORTHOPEDIC	SEEPED	

Mixed-Up Files Vocabulary Word Search 4

```
F P M C A T T R I B U T I N G L S R V N
O H O O A D R T W C S H Y M H F U E E S
O A N U Q P V P N M L E P R X W M G T W
T R O N A U E I U Z K A S A F M A O W
N A T T S M A R S B Q T M C U N O R R
O O O E S F A R B E L R K P O P N D S X
T H N R O D D S R L D I R M E L E I M B
E M Y F C I B I S I M C C A O D D R E N
S R S E I R C S S E E S B I R D R I S S
M M C I A E F T R M D D R M T Y I N N N
U Z R T T C N O M M I A O E H Y Z J Y G
M Y E E E T H W U S O S W D O Z Z U E S
M P E D E F A T C C C S Y P H L S M P
I E C P D D J W U S R E I S E R E T E D
E R H M E Z Y A A F E N N L D K R I R G
S S E R C M S Y L D F D G I I S E C G T
K U D V E M A T I N E E V B C E R E E J
X A H B A R O Q U E Q D U E Z E P Q N D
H D P W S H U F F L I N G R G P B E G Y
D E S C E N D I N G F L A T T E R Y E D
S M U G D A L L O T T E D Y N D G Q R R
```

ADVISED	DECEASED	MATINEE	REGARD
ALLOTTED	DESCENDING	MEDIOCRE	SCOLDING
AMASSED	DIRECTED	MONOTONY	SCREECHED
ASCENDED	DISMISS	MUMMIES	SEEPED
ASSOCIATED	DRIZZLE	MUTUAL	SHUFFLING
ATTRIBUTING	EMERGE	ORTHOPEDIC	SMUG
BAROQUE	FLATTERY	PAUPERS	STOWAWAY
BROWSING	FOOTNOTES	PEER	SUMMONED
CAPER	INJUSTICE	PERSUADE	THEATRICS
CHAUFFEUR	KEEN	PHARAOH	TYRANNIES
CLAMPED	LIBERTY	PUBLICITY	VETO
COUNTERFEITED	MAIMED	QUARRIED	

Mixed-Up Files Vocabulary Word Search 4 Answer Key

```
F P M C A T T R I B U T I N G         S R V
O H O O A D       C     H Y           U E E
O A N U Q P V P       L E P R         M G T
T R O N A U E I U     A S A           M A O
N A T T S M A R S B   T M C U N       O R
O O O E S S   A R E   R   P O P       N D
T H N R O D D S R   D I   M E L       E I
E   Y F C I     I M C C A O D         D R
S   S E I R     S S E B R I   O       R I S
M   C I A E     T M D R M T H         I N N
U   R T C O M   O I A O E Y Z         Z J G
M   E E T H W   U O S W D O           Z U E
M P E D D E A T C C S   P L           L S M
I E C   D W U R E I   E D             E T E
E R H   E A A F N N L K I             I R
S S E   C   Y L F D G I S             C G
  U D   E   M A T I N E E             E E E
  A     B A R O Q U E   D U E         E P N
  D     S H U F F L I N G R           P Y E
D E S C E N D I N G F L A T T E R Y   E
S M U G D A L L O T T E D     Y   D         R
```

ADVISED	DECEASED	MATINEE	REGARD
ALLOTTED	DESCENDING	MEDIOCRE	SCOLDING
AMASSED	DIRECTED	MONOTONY	SCREECHED
ASCENDED	DISMISS	MUMMIES	SEEPED
ASSOCIATED	DRIZZLE	MUTUAL	SHUFFLING
ATTRIBUTING	EMERGE	ORTHOPEDIC	SMUG
BAROQUE	FLATTERY	PAUPERS	STOWAWAY
BROWSING	FOOTNOTES	PEER	SUMMONED
CAPER	INJUSTICE	PERSUADE	THEATRICS
CHAUFFEUR	KEEN	PHARAOH	TYRANNIES
CLAMPED	LIBERTY	PUBLICITY	VETO
COUNTERFEITED	MAIMED	QUARRIED	

Mixed-Up Files Vocabulary Crossword 1

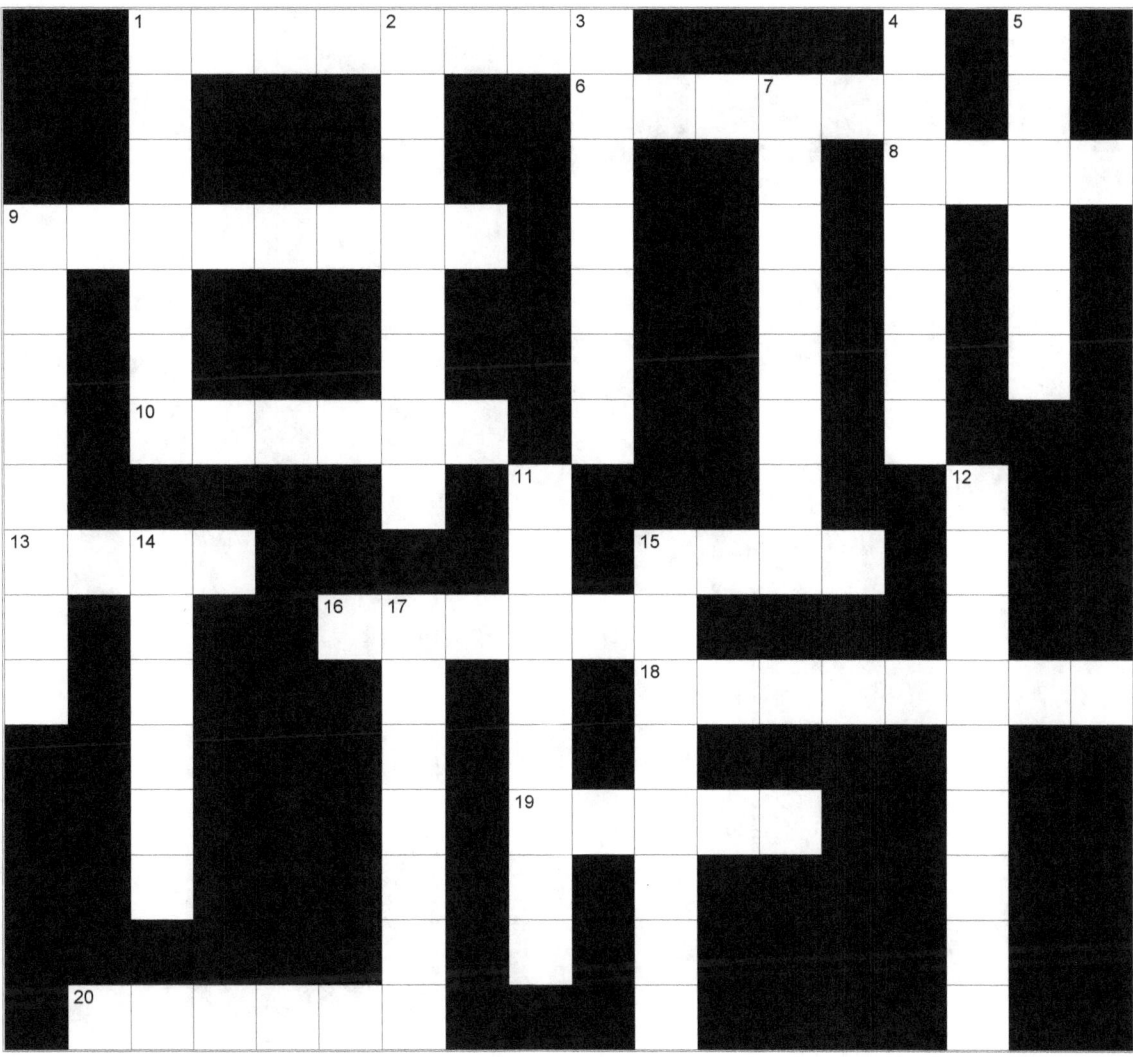

Across
1. Dead
6. To think of a person or thing in a particular way
8. To exercise the right to reject something
9. Sent for someone to come
10. Passed through an opening very slowly
13. Slang term for very cool
15. To look carefully, especially with narrowed eyes
16. Someone who sells something
18. Elaborately or elegantly decorated
19. A light-hearted adventure or a dangerous illegal activity
20. Affected with a severe and permanent injury

Down
1. To officially release students from school
2. Went upward
3. To rain lightly
4. Recommended
5. Shared
7. Precise and correct
9. Characterized by a decrease in size
11. Adequate, but not very good
12. Made a loud, high-pitched sound
14. To appear
15. Urged
17. Revealed

Mixed-Up Files Vocabulary Crossword 1 Answer Key

Across
1. Dead
6. To think of a person or thing in a particular way
8. To exercise the right to reject something
9. Sent for someone to come
10. Passed through an opening very slowly
13. Slang term for very cool
15. To look carefully, especially with narrowed eyes
16. Someone who sells something
18. Elaborately or elegantly decorated
19. A light-hearted adventure or a dangerous illegal activity
20. Affected with a severe and permanent injury

Down
1. To officially release students from school
2. Went upward
3. To rain lightly
4. Recommended
5. Shared
7. Precise and correct
9. Characterized by a decrease in size
11. Adequate, but not very good
12. Made a loud, high-pitched sound
14. To appear
15. Urged
17. Revealed

Mixed-Up Files Vocabulary Crossword 2

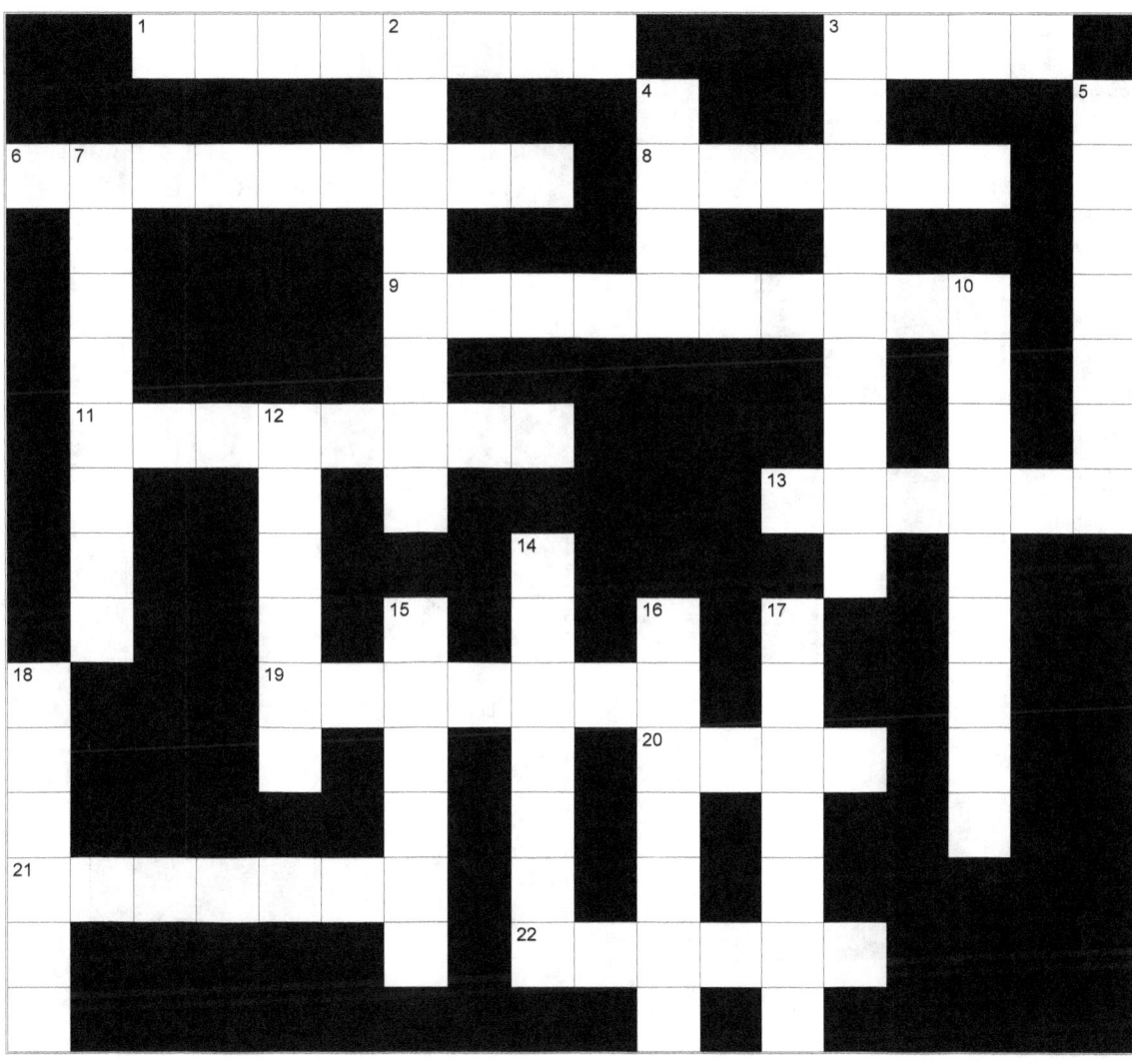

Across
1. Someone who pretends to be someone he is not
3. Conceited
6. Areas of the skin that has been hurt by scraping
8. To appear
9. A young person who has broken the law
11. Sent for someone to come
13. To think of a person or thing in a particular way
19. Collected over time until they form a large fund
20. To exercise the right to reject something
21. To rain lightly
22. Passed through an opening very slowly

Down
2. Complaining, especially when using harsh language
3. Made a loud, high-pitched sound
4. Slang term for very cool
5. Prevented a person from speaking, especially in public
7. Looking around in a leisurely manner
10. Display of false and exaggerated emotion
12. Shared
14. To officially release students from school
15. Affected with a severe and permanent injury
16. Recommended
17. An afternoon performance of a play, usually with cheaper seats than the evening performance
18. Someone who sells something

Mixed-Up Files Vocabulary Crossword 2 Answer Key

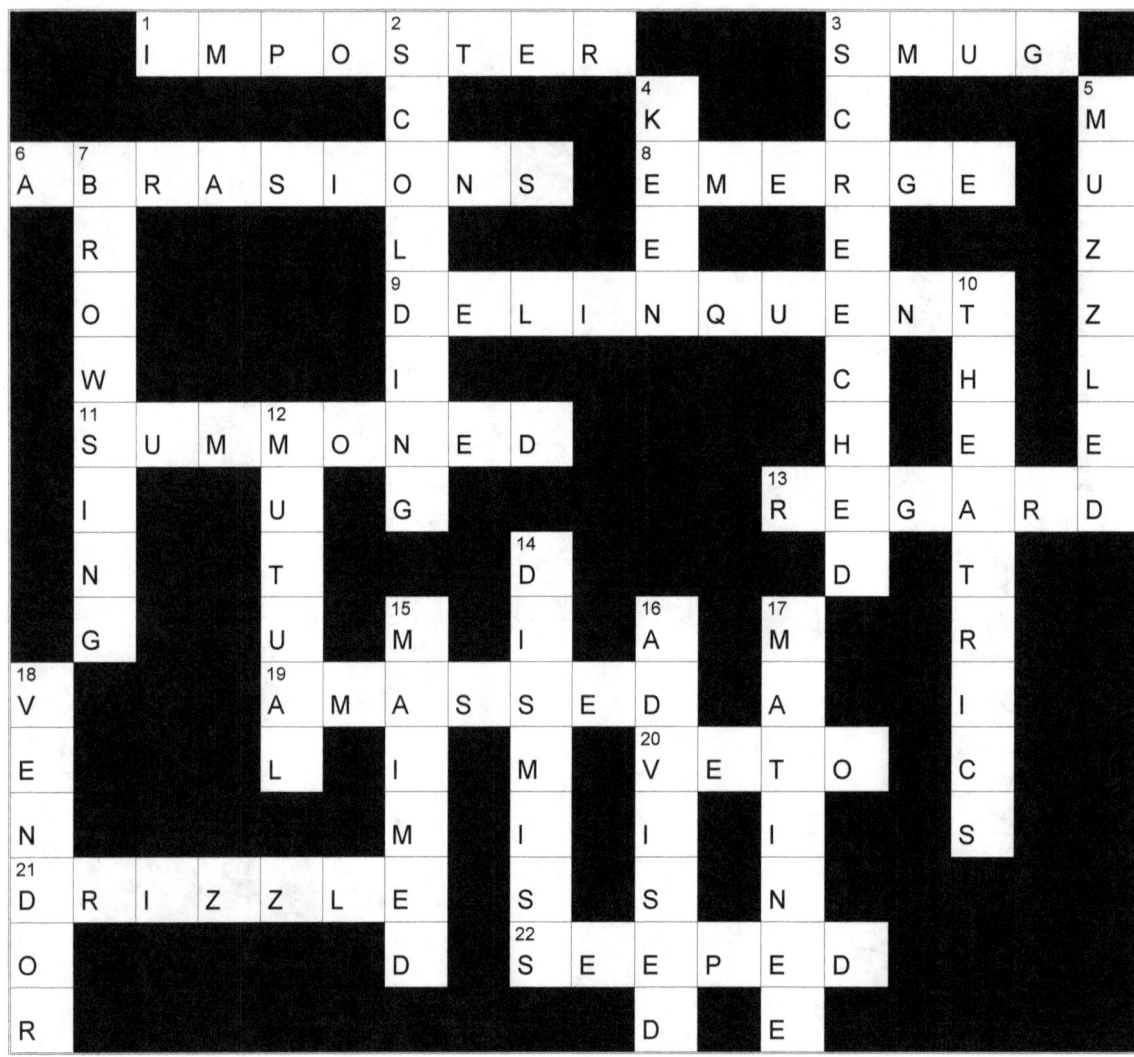

Across
1. Someone who pretends to be someone he is not
3. Conceited
6. Areas of the skin that has been hurt by scraping
8. To appear
9. A young person who has broken the law
11. Sent for someone to come
13. To think of a person or thing in a particular way
19. Collected over time until they form a large fund
20. To exercise the right to reject something
21. To rain lightly
22. Passed through an opening very slowly

Down
2. Complaining, especially when using harsh language
3. Made a loud, high-pitched sound
4. Slang term for very cool
5. Prevented a person from speaking, especially in public
7. Looking around in a leisurely manner
10. Display of false and exaggerated emotion
12. Shared
14. To officially release students from school
15. Affected with a severe and permanent injury
16. Recommended
17. An afternoon performance of a play, usually with cheaper seats than the evening performance
18. Someone who sells something

Mixed-Up Files Vocabulary Crossword 3

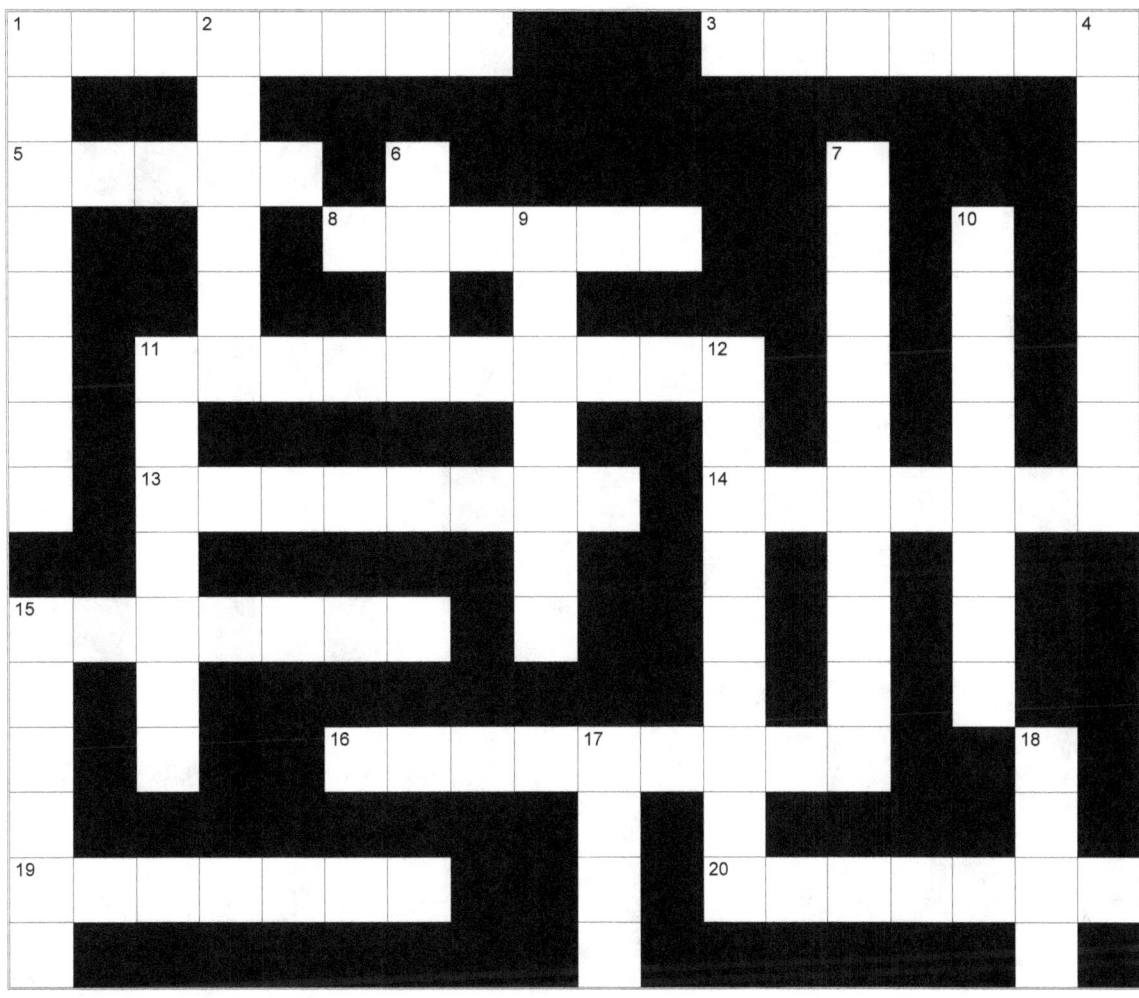

Across
1. Went upward
3. To officially release students from school
5. A light-hearted adventure or a dangerous illegal activity
8. Passed through an opening very slowly
11. A young person who has broken the law
13. Someone who pretends to be someone he is not
14. Revealed
15. Prevented a person from speaking, especially in public
16. Unfair treatment
19. Collected over time until they form a large fund
20. Made a facial expression characterized by drawing the eyebrows together in anger or displeasure

Down
1. Precise and correct
2. To appear
4. Sent for someone to come
6. Slang term for very cool
7. A mixture of several unrelated things
9. Extremely poor individuals
10. Looking around in a leisurely manner
11. To rain lightly
12. Display of false and exaggerated emotion
15. Shared
17. Conceited
18. To look carefully, especially with narrowed eyes

Mixed-Up Files Vocabulary Crossword 3 Answer Key

Across
1. Went upward
3. To officially release students from school
5. A light-hearted adventure or a dangerous illegal activity
8. Passed through an opening very slowly
11. A young person who has broken the law
13. Someone who pretends to be someone he is not
14. Revealed
15. Prevented a person from speaking, especially in public
16. Unfair treatment
19. Collected over time until they form a large fund
20. Made a facial expression characterized by drawing the eyebrows together in anger or displeasure

Down
1. Precise and correct
2. To appear
4. Sent for someone to come
6. Slang term for very cool
7. A mixture of several unrelated things
9. Extremely poor individuals
10. Looking around in a leisurely manner
11. To rain lightly
12. Display of false and exaggerated emotion
15. Shared
17. Conceited
18. To look carefully, especially with narrowed eyes

Mixed-Up Files Vocabulary Crossword 4

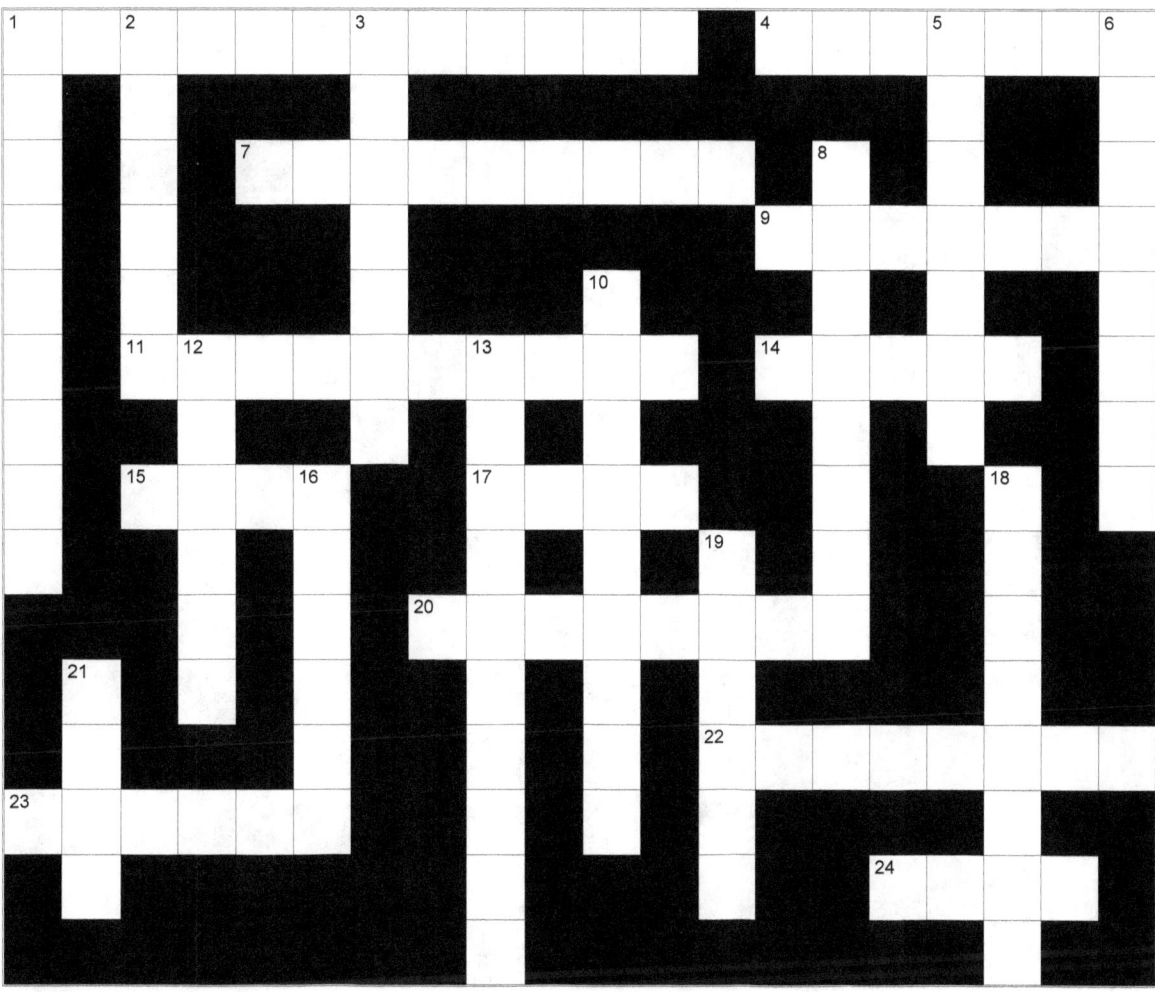

Across
1. Something completed something else, or made it close to perfect
4. Held tightly over
7. To make someone very interested
9. To rain lightly
11. Coming down
14. A light-hearted adventure or a dangerous illegal activity
15. To look carefully, especially with narrowed eyes
17. Conceited
20. The act of complimenting someone for the purpose of getting something
22. In a depressing manner
23. Passed through an opening very slowly
24. To exercise the right to reject something

Down
1. Driver
2. Affected with a severe and permanent injury
3. An afternoon performance of a play, usually with cheaper seats than the evening performance
5. Prevented a person from speaking, especially in public
6. Pointed someone in a particular direction
8. Elaborately or elegantly decorated
10. Unfair treatment
12. To appear
13. Revealing or telling about
16. To think of a person or thing in a particular way
18. A feeling of modesty
19. Someone who sells something
21. Slang term for very cool

Mixed-Up Files Vocabulary Crossword 4 Answer Key

Across
1. Something completed something else, or made it close to perfect
4. Held tightly over
7. To make someone very interested
9. To rain lightly
11. Coming down
14. A light-hearted adventure or a dangerous illegal activity
15. To look carefully, especially with narrowed eyes
17. Conceited
20. The act of complimenting someone for the purpose of getting something
22. In a depressing manner
23. Passed through an opening very slowly
24. To exercise the right to reject something

Down
1. Driver
2. Affected with a severe and permanent injury
3. An afternoon performance of a play, usually with cheaper seats than the evening performance
5. Prevented a person from speaking, especially in public
6. Pointed someone in a particular direction
8. Elaborately or elegantly decorated
10. Unfair treatment
12. To appear
13. Revealing or telling about
16. To think of a person or thing in a particular way
18. A feeling of modesty
19. Someone who sells something
21. Slang term for very cool

Mixed-Up Files Vocabulary Juggle Letters 1

1. GDERAR = 1. _____
   To think of a person or thing in a particular way

2. NOISWRBG = 2. _____
   Looking around in a leisurely manner

3. SDAEEDCE = 3. _____
   Dead

4. AYMSLIDL = 4. _____
   In a depressing manner

5. ATOWWSYA = 5. _____
   Someone who hides on a traveling vessel in hopes of gaining passage without paying

6. NAABSRSIO = 6. _____
   Areas of the skin that has been hurt by scraping

7. DCSTEMUACO = 7. _____
   Become used to a certain thing or way of doing things

8. TIMNEEA = 8. _____
   An afternoon performance of a play, usually with cheaper seats than the evening performance

9. CDERHESCE = 9. _____
   Made a loud, high-pitched sound

10. ATLUMU = 10. _____
    Shared

11. SMIMMUE = 11. _____
    Bodies of people that have been embalmed and wrapped in cloth, as was the custom in ancient Egypt

12. ILCYTPBUI = 12. _____
    Public interest or knowledge

13. MDSMAERTE = 13. _____
    Spoke with many hesitations due to fear or strong emotion

14. DMMIAE = 14. _____
    Affected with a severe and permanent injury

Mixed-Up Files Vocabulary Juggle Letters 1 Answer Key

1. GDERAR = 1. REGARD
   To think of a person or thing in a particular way

2. NOISWRBG = 2. BROWSING
   Looking around in a leisurely manner

3. SDAEEDCE = 3. DECEASED
   Dead

4. AYMSLIDL = 4. DISMALLY
   In a depressing manner

5. ATOWWSYA = 5. STOWAWAY
   Someone who hides on a traveling vessel in hopes of gaining passage without paying

6. NAABSRSIO = 6. ABRASIONS
   Areas of the skin that has been hurt by scraping

7. DCSTEMUACO = 7. ACCUSTOMED
   Become used to a certain thing or way of doing things

8. TIMNEEA = 8. MATINEE
   An afternoon performance of a play, usually with cheaper seats than the evening performance

9. CDERHESCE = 9. SCREECHED
   Made a loud, high-pitched sound

10. ATLUMU = 10. MUTUAL
    Shared

11. SMIMMUE = 11. MUMMIES
    Bodies of people that have been embalmed and wrapped in cloth, as was the custom in ancient Egypt

12. ILCYTPBUI = 12. PUBLICITY
    Public interest or knowledge

13. MDSMAERTE = 13. STAMMERED
    Spoke with many hesitations due to fear or strong emotion

14. DMMIAE = 14. MAIMED
    Affected with a severe and permanent injury

Copyrighted

Mixed-Up Files Vocabulary Juggle Letters 2

1. RHEATTCSI   = 1. _____
                     Display of false and exaggerated emotion

2. DANEESDC   = 2. _____
                     Went upward

3. IMAETEN   = 3. _____
                     An afternoon performance of a play, usually with cheaper seats than the evening performance

4. NRERSODATPT   = 4. _____
                     Moved someone or something from one place to another, especially in a vehicle

5. ANETYLRO   = 5. _____
                     Elaborately or elegantly decorated

6. SRIPTMOE   = 6. _____
                     Someone who pretends to be someone he is not

7. ENIRTIUDG   = 7. _____
                     To make someone very interested

8. EDIRNETOECTUF   = 8. _____
                     Made a realistic copy of

9. OTSWYAWA   = 9. _____
                     Someone who hides on a traveling vessel in hopes of gaining passage without paying

10. TASMAAB   =10. _____
                     An ancient Egyptian tomb with a flat base, sloping sides, and a flat roof

11. NEECDNGSDI   =11. _____
                     Coming down

12. TLOELADT   =12. _____
                     Gave something to somebody as his or her share of what is available

13. ADUEPESR   =13. _____
                     To convince or make someone believe something

14. TAYLTFER   =14. _____
                     The act of complimenting someone for the purpose of getting something

Mixed-Up Files Vocabulary Juggle Letters 2 Answer Key

1. RHEATTCSI = 1. THEATRICS
   Display of false and exaggerated emotion

2. DANEESDC = 2. ASCENDED
   Went upward

3. IMAETEN = 3. MATINEE
   An afternoon performance of a play, usually with cheaper seats than the evening performance

4. NRERSODATPT = 4. TRANSPORTED
   Moved someone or something from one place to another, especially in a vehicle

5. ANETYLRO = 5. ORNATELY
   Elaborately or elegantly decorated

6. SRIPTMOE = 6. IMPOSTER
   Someone who pretends to be someone he is not

7. ENIRTIUDG = 7. INTRIGUED
   To make someone very interested

8. EDIRNETOECTUF = 8. COUNTERFEITED
   Made a realistic copy of

9. OTSWYAWA = 9. STOWAWAY
   Someone who hides on a traveling vessel in hopes of gaining passage without paying

10. TASMAAB = 10. MASTABA
    An ancient Egyptian tomb with a flat base, sloping sides, and a flat roof

11. NEECDNGSDI = 11. DESCENDING
    Coming down

12. TLOELADT = 12. ALLOTTED
    Gave something to somebody as his or her share of what is available

13. ADUEPESR = 13. PERSUADE
    To convince or make someone believe something

14. TAYLTFER = 14. FLATTERY
    The act of complimenting someone for the purpose of getting something

Mixed-Up Files Vocabulary Juggle Letters 3

1. EEKN = 1. _____
Slang term for very cool

2. EOTV = 2. _____
To exercise the right to reject something

3. LEZIDRZ = 3. _____
To rain lightly

4. ABSATMA = 4. _____
An ancient Egyptian tomb with a flat base, sloping sides, and a flat roof

5. NSSIAOARB = 5. _____
Areas of the skin that has been hurt by scraping

6. CSELWDO = 6. _____
Made a facial expression characterized by drawing the eyebrows together in anger or displeasure

7. VIESADD = 7. _____
Recommended

8. IGDSCILONS = 8. _____
Revealing or telling about

9. UTMUAL = 9. _____
Shared

10. RRADUQIE =10. _____
Obtained or gotten after much effort

11. EEDDSRPEHH =11. _____
Guided a group of people or animals

12. UTERAACC =12. _____
Precise and correct

13. DCTEPOELMNME =13. _____
Something completed something else, or made it close to perfect

14. MYITHILU =14. _____
A feeling of modesty

Copyrighted

Mixed-Up Files Vocabulary Juggle Letters 3 Answer Key

1. EEKN = 1. KEEN
Slang term for very cool

2. EOTV = 2. VETO
To exercise the right to reject something

3. LEZIDRZ = 3. DRIZZLE
To rain lightly

4. ABSATMA = 4. MASTABA
An ancient Egyptian tomb with a flat base, sloping sides, and a flat roof

5. NSSIAOARB = 5. ABRASIONS
Areas of the skin that has been hurt by scraping

6. CSELWDO = 6. SCOWLED
Made a facial expression characterized by drawing the eyebrows together in anger or displeasure

7. VIESADD = 7. ADVISED
Recommended

8. IGDSCILONS = 8. DISCLOSING
Revealing or telling about

9. UTMUAL = 9. MUTUAL
Shared

10. RRADUQIE =10. QUARRIED
Obtained or gotten after much effort

11. EEDDSRPEHH =11. SHEPHERDED
Guided a group of people or animals

12. UTERAACC =12. ACCURATE
Precise and correct

13. DCTEPOELMNME =13. COMPLEMENTED
Something completed something else, or made it close to perfect

14. MYITHILU =14. HUMILITY
A feeling of modesty

Mixed-Up Files Vocabulary Juggle Letters 4

1. DIERETDC = 1. _____
Pointed someone in a particular direction

2. PGEDOOGHDE = 2. _____
A mixture of several unrelated things

3. XPSEODE = 3. _____
Revealed

4. SSCTAEADIO = 4. _____
Connected to or having to do with

5. PRUSPEA = 5. _____
Extremely poor individuals

6. UITPCYLIB = 6. _____
Public interest or knowledge

7. MEMMSIU = 7. _____
Bodies of people that have been embalmed and wrapped in cloth, as was the custom in ancient Egypt

8. ENEOCDTEFUTIR = 8. _____
Made a realistic copy of

9. OQEABRU = 9. _____
An ornamental style of European art (mid-16th to early 18th centuries)

10. WDCLSOE =10. _____
Made a facial expression characterized by drawing the eyebrows together in anger or displeasure

11. SIDCGNEEDN =11. _____
Coming down

12. TOEV =12. _____
To exercise the right to reject something

13. MADEOCTCSU =13. _____
Become used to a certain thing or way of doing things

14. RLZIZED =14. _____
To rain lightly

Mixed-Up Files Vocabulary Juggle Letters 4 Answer Key

1. DIERETDC = 1. DIRECTED
Pointed someone in a particular direction

2. PGEDOOGHDE = 2. HODGEPODGE
A mixture of several unrelated things

3. XPSEODE = 3. EXPOSED
Revealed

4. SSCTAEADIO = 4. ASSOCIATED
Connected to or having to do with

5. PRUSPEA = 5. PAUPERS
Extremely poor individuals

6. UITPCYLIB = 6. PUBLICITY
Public interest or knowledge

7. MEMMSIU = 7. MUMMIES
Bodies of people that have been embalmed and wrapped in cloth, as was the custom in ancient Egypt

8. ENEOCDTEFUTIR = 8. COUNTERFEITED
Made a realistic copy of

9. OQEABRU = 9. BAROQUE
An ornamental style of European art (mid-16th to early 18th centuries)

10. WDCLSOE = 10. SCOWLED
Made a facial expression characterized by drawing the eyebrows together in anger or displeasure

11. SIDCGNEEDN = 11. DESCENDING
Coming down

12. TOEV = 12. VETO
To exercise the right to reject something

13. MADEOCTCSU = 13. ACCUSTOMED
Become used to a certain thing or way of doing things

14. RLZIZED = 14. DRIZZLE
To rain lightly

ABRASIONS	Areas of the skin that has been hurt by scraping
ACCURATE	Precise and correct
ACCUSTOMED	Become used to a certain thing or way of doing things
ADVISED	Recommended
ALLOTTED	Gave something to somebody as his or her share of what is available
AMASSED	Collected over time until they form a large fund

ASCENDED	Went upward
ASSOCIATED	Connected to or having to do with
ATTRIBUTING	Giving credit to a person for a particular piece of art or work of literature
BAROQUE	An ornamental style of European art (mid-16th to early 18th centuries)
BROWSING	Looking around in a leisurely manner
CAPER	A light-hearted adventure or a dangerous illegal activity

CHAUFFEUR	Driver
CLAMPED	Held tightly over
COMMOTION	Noisy activity or confusion
COMPLEMENTED	Something completed something else, or made it close to perfect
COUNTERED	To say something that contradicts what someone else has said
COUNTERFEITED	Made a realistic copy of

DECEASED	Dead
DELINQUENT	A young person who has broken the law
DESCENDING	Coming down
DIRECTED	Pointed someone in a particular direction
DISCLOSING	Revealing or telling about
DISMALLY	In a depressing manner

DISMISS	To officially release students from school
DRIZZLE	To rain lightly
EMERGE	To appear
EXPOSED	Revealed
FLATTERY	The act of complimenting someone for the purpose of getting something
FOOTNOTES	An explanation at the bottom of a page giving further information about something in the text above

HODGEPODGE	A mixture of several unrelated things
HUMILITY	A feeling of modesty
IMPOSTER	Someone who pretends to be someone he is not
INJUSTICE	Unfair treatment
INTRIGUED	To make someone very interested
KEEN	Slang term for very cool

LIBERTY	Freedom to think or act
MAIMED	Affected with a severe and permanent injury
MASTABA	An ancient Egyptian tomb with a flat base, sloping sides, and a flat roof
MATINEE	An afternoon performance of a play, usually with cheaper seats than the evening performance
MEDIOCRE	Adequate, but not very good
MONOTONY	boredom that comes from doing the same thing over and over

MUMMIES	Bodies of people that have been embalmed and wrapped in cloth, as was the custom in ancient Egypt
MUTUAL	Shared
MUZZLED	Prevented a person from speaking, especially in public
ORNATELY	Elaborately or elegantly decorated
ORTHOPEDIC	Relating to disorders of the bones, joints, ligaments, or muscles
PAUPERS	Extremely poor individuals

PEER	To look carefully, especially with narrowed eyes
PERSUADE	To convince or make someone believe something
PHARAOH	A king of ancient Egypt
PREOCCUPIED	Totally absorbed in doing or thinking about something else
PROMPTED	Urged
PUBLICITY	Public interest or knowledge

PUNCTUATED	To end with emphasis
QUARRIED	Obtained or gotten after much effort
REGARD	To think of a person or thing in a particular way
SARCOPHAGUS	An ancient stone or marble coffin
SCOLDING	Complaining, especially when using harsh language
SCOWLED	Made a facial expression characterized by drawing the eyebrows together in anger

SCREECHED	Made a loud, high-pitched sound
SEEPED	Passed through an opening very slowly
SHEPHERDED	Guided a group of people or animals
SHRUNKEN	Characterized by a decrease in size
SHUFFLING	To walk without picking up one's feet
SMUG	Conceited

STAMMERED	Spoke with many hesitations due to fear or strong emotion
STEALTHILY	Secretively or cunningly
STOWAWAY	Someone who hides on a traveling vessel in hopes of gaining passage without paying
SUMMONED	Sent for someone to come
THEATRICS	Display of false and exaggerated emotion
TRANSPORTED	Moved someone or something from one place to another, especially in a vehicle

TYRANNIES	Cruelties suffered at the hand of people in authority
VENDOR	Someone who sells something
VETO	To exercise the right to reject something

Mixed-Up Files Vocabulary

SHRUNKEN	MAIMED	INTRIGUED	KEEN	PREOCCUPIED
SCREECHED	ALLOTTED	COMPLEMENTED	THEATRICS	EXPOSED
SHEPHERDED	DISMISS	FREE SPACE	TYRANNIES	MATINEE
MUTUAL	ATTRIBUTING	PAUPERS	SEEPED	SHUFFLING
LIBERTY	COMMOTION	MASTABA	CAPER	DELINQUENT

Mixed-Up Files Vocabulary

PUNCTUATED	CHAUFFEUR	ABRASIONS	MEDIOCRE	REGARD
AMASSED	PEER	STOWAWAY	STAMMERED	PROMPTED
ORTHOPEDIC	DECEASED	FREE SPACE	CLAMPED	MONOTONY
BROWSING	ORNATELY	ADVISED	VETO	COUNTERED
DIRECTED	EMERGE	HUMILITY	ACCUSTOMED	INJUSTICE

Mixed-Up Files Vocabulary

ABRASIONS	PERSUADE	LIBERTY	INTRIGUED	AMASSED
ACCURATE	PHARAOH	KEEN	ORNATELY	COMMOTION
QUARRIED	MEDIOCRE	FREE SPACE	STEALTHILY	BROWSING
PAUPERS	MONOTONY	COUNTERED	SHUFFLING	SMUG
REGARD	IMPOSTER	DECEASED	DELINQUENT	SHRUNKEN

Mixed-Up Files Vocabulary

MUTUAL	ASSOCIATED	SHEPHERDED	PREOCCUPIED	DRIZZLE
SCREECHED	FLATTERY	MUZZLED	VETO	MUMMIES
INJUSTICE	PEER	FREE SPACE	MATINEE	THEATRICS
STOWAWAY	SEEPED	SCOLDING	STAMMERED	PUNCTUATED
DISCLOSING	MASTABA	SARCOPHAGUS	CHAUFFEUR	DESCENDING

Mixed-Up Files Vocabulary

DRIZZLE	PHARAOH	MASTABA	DISMALLY	BROWSING
EMERGE	DECEASED	DIRECTED	STOWAWAY	LIBERTY
TYRANNIES	COUNTERED	FREE SPACE	FOOTNOTES	CHAUFFEUR
HUMILITY	MATINEE	EXPOSED	ORTHOPEDIC	SARCOPHAGUS
ORNATELY	COMMOTION	VETO	STAMMERED	PREOCCUPIED

Mixed-Up Files Vocabulary

ADVISED	KEEN	ATTRIBUTING	ALLOTTED	ASCENDED
FLATTERY	DESCENDING	ABRASIONS	STEALTHILY	SCOWLED
AMASSED	MAIMED	FREE SPACE	PEER	SMUG
COMPLEMENTED	DISCLOSING	SHEPHERDED	PUBLICITY	MUMMIES
SCREECHED	PAUPERS	INTRIGUED	TRANSPORTED	VENDOR

Mixed-Up Files Vocabulary

SHEPHERDED	DISMALLY	SARCOPHAGUS	ORNATELY	MUMMIES
ACCUSTOMED	ABRASIONS	MONOTONY	PHARAOH	ASCENDED
COUNTERFEITED	SCOWLED	FREE SPACE	BROWSING	MUTUAL
DISMISS	EXPOSED	MASTABA	PUNCTUATED	QUARRIED
COUNTERED	COMMOTION	HODGEPODGE	AMASSED	PROMPTED

Mixed-Up Files Vocabulary

VETO	DELINQUENT	ACCURATE	INTRIGUED	SHRUNKEN
PREOCCUPIED	THEATRICS	EMERGE	KEEN	VENDOR
REGARD	MAIMED	FREE SPACE	CAPER	PERSUADE
DESCENDING	FOOTNOTES	BAROQUE	PAUPERS	SMUG
TRANSPORTED	DIRECTED	ADVISED	PUBLICITY	DECEASED

Mixed-Up Files Vocabulary

COUNTERFEITED	ORNATELY	COUNTERED	PHARAOH	MONOTONY
SUMMONED	ACCURATE	SHEPHERDED	INTRIGUED	PEER
DESCENDING	VENDOR	FREE SPACE	KEEN	PERSUADE
FOOTNOTES	INJUSTICE	EXPOSED	MATINEE	SMUG
DISMISS	SCOLDING	MUMMIES	DELINQUENT	DISMALLY

Mixed-Up Files Vocabulary

CHAUFFEUR	DRIZZLE	COMPLEMENTED	ACCUSTOMED	CAPER
TRANSPORTED	MEDIOCRE	MASTABA	ATTRIBUTING	SHRUNKEN
QUARRIED	EMERGE	FREE SPACE	ASCENDED	PREOCCUPIED
VETO	DIRECTED	FLATTERY	BAROQUE	COMMOTION
ALLOTTED	SCREECHED	STOWAWAY	IMPOSTER	ASSOCIATED

Mixed-Up Files Vocabulary

PROMPTED	COMPLEMENTED	STAMMERED	DISCLOSING	MATINEE
DISMALLY	COUNTERFEITED	DIRECTED	SCOLDING	DRIZZLE
COUNTERED	DISMISS	FREE SPACE	MASTABA	EMERGE
PAUPERS	ABRASIONS	HUMILITY	INTRIGUED	STOWAWAY
SUMMONED	THEATRICS	ADVISED	MEDIOCRE	MAIMED

Mixed-Up Files Vocabulary

AMASSED	CHAUFFEUR	ASCENDED	DECEASED	DESCENDING
COMMOTION	QUARRIED	CLAMPED	PUNCTUATED	VETO
BROWSING	ASSOCIATED	FREE SPACE	SARCOPHAGUS	BAROQUE
LIBERTY	DELINQUENT	PHARAOH	MUZZLED	ATTRIBUTING
PREOCCUPIED	MUTUAL	MUMMIES	EXPOSED	PERSUADE

Mixed-Up Files Vocabulary

SEEPED	PUBLICITY	MATINEE	PREOCCUPIED	SMUG
SUMMONED	CLAMPED	STAMMERED	STOWAWAY	MUTUAL
CAPER	PUNCTUATED	FREE SPACE	ASSOCIATED	DISMALLY
ALLOTTED	HUMILITY	MONOTONY	ATTRIBUTING	DECEASED
DRIZZLE	SCOWLED	COUNTERED	PERSUADE	SHUFFLING

Mixed-Up Files Vocabulary

REGARD	TRANSPORTED	SARCOPHAGUS	IMPOSTER	BAROQUE
LIBERTY	PEER	SHRUNKEN	MUZZLED	MEDIOCRE
DIRECTED	TYRANNIES	FREE SPACE	COMPLEMENTED	VETO
ASCENDED	SHEPHERDED	SCOLDING	INTRIGUED	CHAUFFEUR
DISCLOSING	PAUPERS	ABRASIONS	ACCURATE	VENDOR

Mixed-Up Files Vocabulary

KEEN	TYRANNIES	MATINEE	INJUSTICE	COUNTERFEITED
FLATTERY	ACCUSTOMED	STAMMERED	STEALTHILY	IMPOSTER
PUNCTUATED	SEEPED	FREE SPACE	PHARAOH	SMUG
CHAUFFEUR	VETO	COMPLEMENTED	ADVISED	MUZZLED
DISMISS	PUBLICITY	CAPER	CLAMPED	MAIMED

Mixed-Up Files Vocabulary

PAUPERS	ACCURATE	DISMALLY	PREOCCUPIED	DISCLOSING
LIBERTY	SHUFFLING	MASTABA	PERSUADE	QUARRIED
MUMMIES	REGARD	FREE SPACE	MONOTONY	INTRIGUED
SUMMONED	STOWAWAY	MUTUAL	SCREECHED	PEER
COUNTERED	PROMPTED	ORNATELY	BROWSING	ASSOCIATED

Mixed-Up Files Vocabulary

HODGEPODGE	FLATTERY	MUZZLED	COUNTERFEITED	LIBERTY
TRANSPORTED	COMPLEMENTED	SARCOPHAGUS	EXPOSED	DRIZZLE
COUNTERED	ABRASIONS	FREE SPACE	CAPER	VETO
SCOLDING	SCOWLED	ADVISED	DESCENDING	MUTUAL
REGARD	ASCENDED	CHAUFFEUR	DISCLOSING	DELINQUENT

Mixed-Up Files Vocabulary

DISMISS	AMASSED	HUMILITY	SUMMONED	ASSOCIATED
MASTABA	IMPOSTER	MEDIOCRE	PAUPERS	SHUFFLING
PUNCTUATED	ACCUSTOMED	FREE SPACE	COMMOTION	DISMALLY
CLAMPED	SCREECHED	BAROQUE	SMUG	FOOTNOTES
SHEPHERDED	STOWAWAY	EMERGE	MONOTONY	MATINEE

Mixed-Up Files Vocabulary

DRIZZLE	PUBLICITY	COMPLEMENTED	MATINEE	INTRIGUED
EMERGE	IMPOSTER	DELINQUENT	VENDOR	AMASSED
HUMILITY	ABRASIONS	FREE SPACE	MAIMED	ORNATELY
ACCURATE	STOWAWAY	SEEPED	PHARAOH	MASTABA
PAUPERS	ASCENDED	ATTRIBUTING	SCREECHED	FLATTERY

Mixed-Up Files Vocabulary

SCOLDING	PUNCTUATED	COUNTERED	TRANSPORTED	PREOCCUPIED
CAPER	MEDIOCRE	DIRECTED	COMMOTION	SHEPHERDED
MONOTONY	REGARD	FREE SPACE	SHUFFLING	STAMMERED
HODGEPODGE	LIBERTY	DESCENDING	DISMISS	DECEASED
DISMALLY	EXPOSED	BAROQUE	PROMPTED	ACCUSTOMED

Mixed-Up Files Vocabulary

SHEPHERDED	SEEPED	PAUPERS	ORNATELY	DELINQUENT
STOWAWAY	REGARD	LIBERTY	DISMALLY	PUBLICITY
INTRIGUED	KEEN	FREE SPACE	ASSOCIATED	STEALTHILY
SCOLDING	ACCURATE	HODGEPODGE	PREOCCUPIED	STAMMERED
SCREECHED	DRIZZLE	MAIMED	ACCUSTOMED	ABRASIONS

Mixed-Up Files Vocabulary

DESCENDING	BROWSING	INJUSTICE	MATINEE	MASTABA
PUNCTUATED	TRANSPORTED	MUMMIES	ADVISED	DISCLOSING
EMERGE	COMMOTION	FREE SPACE	CAPER	MUTUAL
COUNTERED	FOOTNOTES	SHRUNKEN	PHARAOH	SCOWLED
IMPOSTER	TYRANNIES	SUMMONED	DISMISS	VETO

Mixed-Up Files Vocabulary

SCREECHED	ADVISED	ORNATELY	ASCENDED	LIBERTY
HODGEPODGE	DELINQUENT	COUNTERFEITED	PROMPTED	ORTHOPEDIC
MONOTONY	IMPOSTER	FREE SPACE	FOOTNOTES	MUTUAL
ABRASIONS	TRANSPORTED	BAROQUE	DIRECTED	PREOCCUPIED
COMMOTION	STOWAWAY	MASTABA	ACCURATE	DECEASED

Mixed-Up Files Vocabulary

COMPLEMENTED	CAPER	EMERGE	INTRIGUED	THEATRICS
MATINEE	BROWSING	PUNCTUATED	ALLOTTED	MAIMED
SUMMONED	STEALTHILY	FREE SPACE	SCOLDING	PAUPERS
ATTRIBUTING	KEEN	TYRANNIES	SEEPED	DESCENDING
COUNTERED	MUMMIES	PHARAOH	DISCLOSING	SCOWLED

Mixed-Up Files Vocabulary

DISCLOSING	PHARAOH	ABRASIONS	DELINQUENT	COUNTERFEITED
EXPOSED	COUNTERED	DECEASED	DIRECTED	STOWAWAY
ASSOCIATED	TYRANNIES	FREE SPACE	PUBLICITY	MONOTONY
MAIMED	SEEPED	SARCOPHAGUS	ORTHOPEDIC	STAMMERED
REGARD	MATINEE	COMPLEMENTED	DRIZZLE	THEATRICS

Mixed-Up Files Vocabulary

MASTABA	COMMOTION	DESCENDING	PROMPTED	TRANSPORTED
SHEPHERDED	SMUG	SCOLDING	PAUPERS	SCOWLED
LIBERTY	ACCURATE	FREE SPACE	HUMILITY	FOOTNOTES
PUNCTUATED	PERSUADE	ALLOTTED	FLATTERY	QUARRIED
SCREECHED	BROWSING	DISMISS	PREOCCUPIED	IMPOSTER

Mixed-Up Files Vocabulary

SHEPHERDED	QUARRIED	DELINQUENT	FOOTNOTES	EMERGE
DISMISS	HUMILITY	VETO	PUNCTUATED	ORNATELY
COUNTERED	VENDOR	FREE SPACE	INJUSTICE	TYRANNIES
TRANSPORTED	THEATRICS	COMPLEMENTED	ABRASIONS	SCOLDING
DIRECTED	BROWSING	ORTHOPEDIC	MUZZLED	ACCUSTOMED

Mixed-Up Files Vocabulary

CAPER	BAROQUE	DISCLOSING	SHUFFLING	PUBLICITY
CHAUFFEUR	ALLOTTED	PROMPTED	INTRIGUED	COMMOTION
CLAMPED	SUMMONED	FREE SPACE	LIBERTY	DECEASED
HODGEPODGE	AMASSED	SHRUNKEN	COUNTERFEITED	PEER
SCREECHED	MATINEE	MUMMIES	SMUG	PAUPERS

Mixed-Up Files Vocabulary

SHUFFLING	LIBERTY	DRIZZLE	ALLOTTED	COUNTERED
CLAMPED	CAPER	SCOWLED	PAUPERS	DECEASED
MASTABA	ORNATELY	FREE SPACE	PEER	KEEN
DISMALLY	ASSOCIATED	TYRANNIES	BROWSING	DELINQUENT
MEDIOCRE	SMUG	IMPOSTER	DISMISS	ABRASIONS

Mixed-Up Files Vocabulary

VETO	BAROQUE	AMASSED	SCREECHED	MUMMIES
COMPLEMENTED	PREOCCUPIED	PUBLICITY	ACCUSTOMED	INTRIGUED
SHEPHERDED	HODGEPODGE	FREE SPACE	MONOTONY	DISCLOSING
EXPOSED	PROMPTED	INJUSTICE	DIRECTED	SCOLDING
HUMILITY	COMMOTION	DESCENDING	THEATRICS	MUZZLED

Mixed-Up Files Vocabulary

KEEN	QUARRIED	ORNATELY	FOOTNOTES	DISCLOSING
LIBERTY	ORTHOPEDIC	DIRECTED	CLAMPED	MUZZLED
EMERGE	TYRANNIES	FREE SPACE	MASTABA	COMPLEMENTED
THEATRICS	CAPER	SCOWLED	MUTUAL	DELINQUENT
INJUSTICE	SHRUNKEN	PHARAOH	VENDOR	ACCUSTOMED

Mixed-Up Files Vocabulary

ADVISED	PERSUADE	PUBLICITY	INTRIGUED	ASSOCIATED
PREOCCUPIED	PROMPTED	BROWSING	MAIMED	ASCENDED
SMUG	HODGEPODGE	FREE SPACE	ABRASIONS	FLATTERY
MEDIOCRE	MUMMIES	PUNCTUATED	DRIZZLE	STOWAWAY
EXPOSED	HUMILITY	SHEPHERDED	AMASSED	SCREECHED

www.ingramcontent.com/pod-product-compliance
Lightning Source LLC
LaVergne TN
LVHW081537060526
838200LV00048B/2115